Turning Home

God, Ghosts
and Human Destiny

Paul F. Eno

Photography and Illustration Credits
Cover by Frank Rivera; p. 12, top photo by L. Joseph Letendre, bottom by the author, Pomfret, Connecticut; p. 14, photo by the author, Pomfret, Connecticut; pp. 43-44, illustrations by the author; p. 54, photo by the author, Uxbridge, Massachusetts; p. 55, photos by Donna Fillie, Torrington, Connecticut; p. 59, photos by the author, Stonington, Connecticut, and Woonsocket, Rhode Island; p. 63, courtesy West Virginia Division of Natural Resources; p. 67, photo by the author; p. 78, left photo by Steve Hitchins, Dendera, Egypt, right photo by the author, from his collection; p. 106, photo by Benjamin Eno, Orange County, Vermont; p. 131, courtesy Lebanese Ministry of Tourism; p. 137, photo by Steve Hitchins, Mohenjo Daro, Pakistan; p. 229, courtesy WNRI Radio, Woonsocket, Rhode Island.

New River Press Web site is: www.newriverpress.com

FIRST EDITION

ISBN   1-891724-06-1
ISBN-13   978-1-891724-06-0

To my beloved wife, Jackie,
in this, our 25th anniversary year!

For your unwavering loyalty, your unending patience,
your undying faith in me, and your endless love
for God, for our children and for me,
thank you!

Contents

Introduction: Who Are You? 4

1. What We Know 11
So Much for the Enlightenment 14
…Anything is Possible! 20
Zero 21

2. From Square One 26
Seminary Ghost Hunters? 28
Out on My Ear 34
'The Haunter' and 'The Children in the Corner' 35
Finding Schroedinger's Cat 40
Turning on the Lights 49
The Case of the Almost Suicide 51
West Virginia Outreach 62
The Paranormal Pooch 66
Ghosts as Teachers 67

3. In the Image and Likeness of Man 70
Belief 71
Ye of Simple Faith 73
Unbelief 74
City Mouse, Country Mouse 75
Mother is Never Forgotten 77
Do All Religions Worship the Same God? 79
Toward the Dawning of the Dawn 80

4. The Quest for the One 83
Meet the Paradox 85
Seeing and Not Seeing 86
The 'New Age' 88
Meet the Fractal 89
Mitochondrial Eve 90
Who Shattered God? 93
Voices from the Dawn of Time 94
Father and Mother 97

5. Enemies: Divide and Conquer 83
The Parasite Factor 102
The Prussian Parasite 109
The God Connection 111
The Bell Witch 114
The Art of the Fall 116

6. Neutrals: The Wrong One **118**
From Unlikely Sources *119*
The Genes that Shouldn't Be There *122*
What Happened? *124*
Multiversal Tourists? *125*
The Elohim Enigma *127*
"In the Image and Likeness of God"? *130*
Wars of the Gods *134*
The Lawgivers *136*
In the Shadow of Mothman *140*
Is There a Devil? *141*

7. Friends: Guides and Guardians **143**
More Angels than Parasites *145*
The Sacred Tetragrammaton *146*
Maryam's Encounter *148*
The Message is in the Miracles *150*
Volunteers from Beyond *151*
Unexpected Neighbors *152*
Garden of Ehden/Eden Revisited? *153*
Ancestors and Loved Ones *154*

8. Death and Life **158**
Is There Really No Death? *161*
'And a Little Child Shall Lead Them....' *162*
All for One, One for All *166*
The Death of Death *169*
What Happens When We Die? *171*
Why the Death Experience at All? *173*

9. Finding God **174**
Say the Word! *175*
Religion, Right or Wrong? *176*
God as Cosmic Teddy Bear *180*
Our Missing Mother *181*
Is God Green or Gray? *182*
Is God Just Us? *184*
Is God All-Natural? *184*
In Our Own Way *186*
Destiny Calls *188*
Moving to Square Two *189*
I Shall Be *189*

10. Connecting the Dots **191**
A Very Long Memory *192*
Step One: Accept *194*
Step Two: Believe *198*
Step Three: Act *199*
Shaking the Multiverse *204*
Final Thoughts *206*
Acknowledgments *209*
Bibliography *210*
Index *216*
The Author *229*

Introduction: Who Are You?

Who are you? Where will you go when you die? Where are your loved ones who already have? Who is God? Why are we the way we are? Why is God the way God is? Is there a God?

You're about the get some unexpected answers. As a matter of fact, you're about to plunge into icy waters few have dared explore in many centuries, to plumb the depths and probe the unseen crannies of an "iceberg" our remote ancestors knew. It's an iceberg most of us arrogant moderns know, however, only by its "tip": campfire ghost stories, tales of "Bigfoot," a pleasant shudder from a Hollywood film, yarns about the UFO seen by the friend of a friend, the occasional psychic or medium who tells us something we already know....

Beneath that "tip," however, is deep knowledge and strange experience that sleep within us still. In the rare moments we're not distracted by the telephone, e-mail, blaring MP3 players or a hundred other things, there will be a second now and then when something in our folklore, an image of God vaguely remembered in our most ancient religious texts, or the way a sunset catches in our minds, will "ring a bell." Then, just for an instant of an instant, we may *know again*. Then it's lost and, tragically, we usually think nothing more about it.

This "iceberg" is what we so blithely call the "paranormal." What is the paranormal?

The term means "beyond the normal." It's any human experience for which there is no "rational" explanation that's mutually agreed upon.

For our purposes the paranormal includes ghosts, poltergeists and any sort of spiritual phenomena; mediumistic and psychic phenomena, including extra-sensory perception (ESP), clairvoyance, clairaudience, *déjà vu*, remote viewing (mentally seeing a place, person or event from a great physical distance), out-of-body and near-death experiences, and the like; reincarnation phenomena; UFOs and "close encounters"; unknown or unexplained, out-of-place animals (known as "cryptids"); displacements or slips in time and space; and appearing or disappearing people, places or things for which there's no explanation.

The renowned parapsychologist (one with special academic credentials who studies mediumistic and psychic phenomena) Rhea White (1931-) refers to anything paranormal as "exceptional human experience." But after half a lifetime investigating it – indeed, living with it – I'm utterly convinced that "paranormal" is a complete misnomer. The paranormal is entirely normal. With the greatest respect to Dr. White, it's not "exceptional" at all.

As we scurry about our little affairs every day, the paranormal forms the half-suspected background. It looms over and under every moment of our lives; every aspect of our days; everything we think, believe, were, are and will be. It dominates our history. It constitutes our subconscious minds and motivates our conscious minds.

The paranormal is the mother of both religion and science. It is God's blueprint for what truly constitutes reality. It is the fount of wonder.

Even more, I believe that understanding the paranormal is our key to understanding God, the universe, each other, ourselves and, most of all, death. It is the beginning and ending of all questions. If we are to cease being blind, and if our modern minds are to unshrivel from centuries of cynicism and doubt, we must learn to accept, believe and, yes, use the paranormal.

The paranormal is the key to human destiny, to our success or failure as a species. But even if we accept the existence of the paranormal, with all its implications, how and how much can we actually use it? Can we as individuals and as a species use the paranormal to help navigate past the terrors that scar the modern world? Can ghosts, poltergeists and other "unexplained mysteries" – things most people either don't believe in or are terrified of – somehow point the way toward better lives for all of us? Can acknowledging and embracing what's really behind these mysteries, as our ancestors did, actually help bring the human race together?

Yes and yes!

I think we need to retrace our steps, to find what we've lost, to go back to what we all have in common. And that commonality lies in the universal experience of every culture, every nation, every person. It's what first led our remote ancestors to seek the "how" and "why" of the universe. It's what first prodded them to ponder the enigma of death. It's what led them to cry to God to save them.

I suspect that it's also what first divided people from each other, turned God into myriad gods, and spurred the birth of the earliest civilizations.

It's the paranormal and what can come out of it – good or

bad. Through the paranormal, we can touch both the divine and the demonic, and we can learn what we really are.

The paranormal *is* the "big picture."

In this book I try to share a boundless vision of the universe I and many others have glimpsed through long experience with the paranormal. It's a universe full of friends and enemies, a universe our ancestors knew, and it's a universe to which we must turn together if we are to rediscover ourselves, avert disaster for our planet, and take our species to the next step in its evolution.

I've sometimes been criticized for "trying to explain everything." People say things like, "Let it go. Some things just can't be explained."

I don't believe that at all. I believe that everything can be explained. But it's *in the explanations* that the mystery, the wonder and the glory truly are! There will always be unanswered questions, but will we have the courage and the imagination to embrace the answers?

Whatever happens afterward, it's time to turn back to "square one." It's time to turn home.

Paul F. Eno
Town's End, 2006

Believe

1

What We Know

Ignorance is the curse of God,
Knowledge the wing wherewith we fly to heaven....
     -William Shakespeare, from *Henry VI*

All seven of us heard it at the same moment on that chilly fall day in 1971. For most of the past 5,000 years, and who knows how many silent epochs before that, it would have been a simple, everyday sound. But amid the haunted woods of northeast Connecticut on this Halloween weekend, it gripped with awe and disbelief the fellow seminary students and corporate photo expert who were with me.

It was the rumble of an oxcart – an *invisible* oxcart — bumping along a rutted road that had long since vanished beneath an impossible tangle of hardwoods and vines. As we stood, dumbfounded, the sound grew louder and closer. From less than thirty feet away came the jingle of harnesses, the heavy hoofbeats, the clatter of wooden wheels. Two of us stepped toward the sound, but stopped when we heard a man's voice. "Hya! Hya!" hollered the unseen driver, and there shot through the air what

Above, part of the 1971 "Village of Voices" investigating team. The author is at the far left. Below, the area where the invisible oxcart was heard, taken several months earlier.

sounded like the crack of a whip. A few long moments later the sounds faded off to the right, down a trail into what was, in 1971, a swamp.

We were young "ghost hunters," it was our first investigation of an alleged haunting, and we had seen and heard things in this place that we thought only Hollywood could dream up. We stood in shock amid the overgrown cellar holes, stone walls and woods of the settlement that had been known to its Welsh-born founders as *Bara Hack*, roughly translated from the Cymric language as "the place where we break bread." Established in the 1770s and depopulated, supposedly, by disease late in the 19th century, *Bara Hack* had long been known locally as "The Village of Voices."

Written accounts from as far back as the 1920s reported frequent paranormal activity there, and they weren't kidding. Our 1971 team consisted of six of us from St. Thomas Seminary in Bloomfield, Connecticut, all sixteen to eighteen years old, and a photo expert from an East Hartford technology firm. In our four expeditions to *Bara Hack* that year and the year after, we experienced apparitions, teleportation (the movement of objects from one place to another by non-physical means), and numerous photographic and auditory anomalies. For long periods we would hear all around us what we could only conclude were the sounds of daily life in that long-vanished village: farm tools, cows, dogs, snatches of conversation....

The Village of Voices. The case is fully recounted in my 1998 book *Faces at the Window: First Hand Accounts of the Paranormal in New England.*

In my ensuing decades as a paranormal investigator, I would experience far more bizarre sights and sounds than I had at *Bara Hack*. I was to be injured by poltergeists, insulted and taunted by nonhuman voices, stalked by "spirit orbs," and touched by presences that I can only describe as angelic or even divine.

The village cemetery at **Bara Hack** *in 1971.*

But *Bara Hack* was the beginning, the place that has "rocked my world" from that day until this.

So Much for the Enlightenment

Before we begin any journey into the unexplained, especially one with the ultimate destination that I suggest, we have to accept the fact that the paranormal is real. That's not an easy task for modern minds, molded and painfully narrowed by the thoughts and perceptions of the 18th century "Enlightenment." In that period European and American thinkers rejected the "superstitions" of past ages, replacing them with a scientific rigor based on the belief that the whole universe is essentially a machine based entirely on matter. If you could study and understand the *parts* of something, whether it be a plant cell, a human body, the Earth or the entire universe, you could understand the whole. From this mechanistic science came the attitude we were all trained to believe: If you can't materially see it, touch it, taste it, smell it or hear it, it can't exist.

This approach to science works when we're building a house or planning a new highway, but it has never worked when it comes to explaining what the universe really is. That's because the universe is neither mechanistic nor entirely material.

For generations we westerners were taught, as soon as we left childhood, to disbelieve in anything beyond the material world. We usually managed to work religion in there somewhere, but we rarely let it interfere with our daily lives because God was as divided from us as we were from each other. We learned to disbelieve even our senses when they didn't perceive things that agreed with our comfortable, secure, man-is-in-charge view of the world.

Many people caught (and many still have) what I call "skepticemia," an almost pathological need *not* to believe in anything beyond matter. They react with great insecurity, a terrible closed-mindedness, and even anger when confronted with evidence of the paranormal.

Enlightenment science gave us a new world with lots of cool gadgets, great medicines, and nice creature comforts. But because it encouraged a pitifully incomplete view of the universe, it finished a robbery of our souls and our human heritage started by "others" millennia before. This machine-science also encouraged a false and ferocious individualism that tore us from one another. It created a civilization with amnesia, and it allowed us to justify trashing the planet. We have become the richest, angriest, loneliest, most cynical, most identity-challenged, most spoiled, most unbelieving, and truly the saddest people in human history. That's why we get so frustrated with ourselves and each other without really knowing why.

Of course, for those who accept the fact that they're experiencing it, the paranormal is as real as a two-edged sword: It has a good side and a bad side. But it can be, for better or worse, life-transforming. The theories, explanations and details may differ, but to those whose homes and lives have been shattered by the tantrums of a poltergeist, who have shrieked in terror at the sight of "Bigfoot" peering through their trailer windows, or have known the tender touch of a departed loved one, the experience is undeniable and unforgettable. And it lets us know that there's much, much more to the universe and to ourselves than Enlightenment science could begin to describe.

In life, real fear and true frustration come only when we refuse to accept, believe and understand this.

"Why do you doubt your senses?" moans the ghost of Jacob Marley to Ebenezer Scrooge in Charles Dickens's *A Christmas Carol.*

"Because," says Scrooge, "a little thing affects them. A slight disorder of the stomach makes them cheats. You may be an undigested bit of beef, a blot of mustard, a crumb of cheese, a fragment of an underdone potato. There's more of gravy than of grave about you, whatever you are!"

Scrooge had skepticemia: If it doesn't fit our narrow, predictable worldview, then many of us won't believe it even if it floats up and punches us in the nose. That invisible oxcart driver at *Bara Hack* must have been mass hysteria, some sort of temporal lobe epilepsy shared by seven suggestible people, or an undigested bit of pizza.

I'm often asked, "What can we do to prove scientifically that the paranormal exists?" My answer: "Absolutely nothing."

Why not? Because of the nature of the modern mind: For the believer, no proof is necessary; for the unbeliever, no proof is enough. There is nothing any paranormal investigator can do to "prove" anything to mainstream science. For one thing, when it comes to the paranormal, eyewitness accounts never seem to constitute "scientific evidence." The implication is that anyone who has a paranormal encounter must have bad eyesight, poor hearing, impaired judgment, addled thinking, a drug dependency, or all five. Strange that in courts of law the first thing lawyers look for is eyewitnesses!

Another problem: The paranormal is the outward manifestation of what can only be called a multi-dimensional reality. It can't be stuffed into a laboratory to be tested and replicated according to an Enlightenment-era scientific method (observation, theory, experiment, law) designed to describe only a three-dimensional, mechanistic world.

When the American Society for Psychical Research (ASPR) was founded in 1885, it involved many scholars, philosophers, doctors and students of the new science of psychology. These men had the courage to consider the paranormal possible, and they wanted to explain it by probing the human mind in new ways. The result was the modern science (some still say pseudoscience) of parapsychology, a Rodney Dangerfield among academic disciplines if ever there was one.

Parapsychology is the study of the evidence for mental awareness beyond the five accepted senses, or of mental influence over material objects without action from known physical means. Its practitioners have tried for decades to study psychic phenomena (extra-sensory perception or ESP, remote viewing, telekinesis, etc.) in an acceptably scientific way. Joseph B. Rhine (1895-1980), the founder of modern parapsychology, and those who came after him, dared not only to ask questions like: "Is there life after death?" They sought to take the question out of the hands of psychics, mediums and cultists, then apply strict scientific principles to answering it. Louisa E. Rhine (1891-1983), J.B.'s wife, whom I had the honor of knowing, worked doggedly to categorize phenomena in a scientific way. She pioneered the study of ESP in children and the elderly.

From the 1930s through the 1970s there were some interesting results both in and out of the laboratory, but nothing the general scientific community would accept as "statistically significant," and certainly not as "proof" of the existence of the paranormal. Even today only a few accredited colleges and universities offer courses, let alone degrees, in parapsychology. As might be expected from the unbelievers for whom no proof is enough, parapsychology has always been a lightning rod for criticism when it comes to its experimental controls, statistical significance of data, and alleged instances of fraud, coincidence or suggestibility.

Most early parapsychologists assumed that there was a way to explain the paranormal, psychic phenomena in particular, with standard scientific principles that just hadn't been discovered yet. Within a century, however, most leading members of the ASPR had realized that there was more to the paranormal than met the electrode and the lab coat. Today many major players in the ASPR have embraced pioneering ideas such as transpersonal psychology (which studies transcendent and spiritual human experiences) and, to a degree, the jaw-dropping branch of physics known as quantum mechanics or quantum physics.

Quantum physics is turning our understanding of reality upside down, and it's the key element in this book.

Nevertheless, not even real scientists have had much luck persuading other real scientists that the paranormal exists in any significant way.

What I truly resent about skepticemics, scientists or not, is their implied disrespect for our ancestors. Their attitude says that most of our predecessor cultures were made up of uneducated nitwits because they took for granted things like God, an afterlife, the connectedness of all things, and the paranormal. It also implies that I, and everyone who has witnessed phenomena with me over the past thirty-six years, am delusional.

Science is not the answer to our questions or our problems. Virtually every scientific discovery poses more questions than it answers, and many theories and even laws of science past have been overturned by subsequent discoveries. Scientists in most every field are at each other's throats over one "fact" or another. The scientific method itself is being shaken by the mind-blowing insights of quantum physics, where space and time are the same thing, past and future have no objective reality, and effects can take place before causes.

There's yet another dimension to the problems of science today. The public perceives scientists as hard-working, honest (if eccentric) people in lab coats, laboring away in basements and cluttered laboratories for the benefit of humanity. That may have been the general case in days of yore, and it may be the isolated case now. But this is the 21st century, and it's all about bucks. And the bucks come primarily from two sources: governments and corporations.

Governments' primary concern is preserving themselves, come what may. This means mucho moola for defense and national security. Scientists who play the game, perfect the weapons and accessories, and don't come up with uncomfortable data (such as this or that secret government activity causing cancer) are the ones who get the money. Those who speak out or come up with inconvenient conclusions get cut off, ridiculed and sometimes even blackballed or jailed.

Governments love to spend money; corporations love to make money. They do that with "scientific proof" that this drug prevents heart disease, this car is safer, or this detergent gets your undies whiter. When they hire "independent laboratories" to come up with findings, they expect beneficial results (beneficial for them).

University labs aren't the paragons of virtue people think they are either. They get hired for many government and corporate studies, and they're more than happy to deliver.

No benefits, no bucks. Scientists have human failings too. While mainstream science doesn't believe in the paranormal, it does when there's money to be made. From 1970 to about 1995, and maybe all the way to today for all I know, the American military poured a least $20 million into a project to pin down and perfect elements of paranormal warfare. Called, believe it or not, "Project Star Gate," the program and others like it were a Cold War response to a similar Soviet program. The goal was to recruit and train psychics to discern enemy plans and intentions, locate spies and weapons by "remote viewing," and even create fires, explosions, weather disturbances, and other forms of clandestine attack from a distance.

It reminds me of character Winston Zedimore's line in the 1984 film *Ghostbusters*. "If there's a steady paycheck in it, I'll believe anything you say!"

I understand that the Pentagon has had some success in these experiments and that they're still going on. And I believe that if any government really has developed military applications for the paranormal, its leaders and scientists must be vividly aware of the nature of reality as you'll read about it in this book.

...Anything is Possible!

Don't get me wrong about science. I'll always love, respect and be a student of all sciences, when it really is science and not politics. I'll always try to be an *open-minded* skeptic. In the words of the great author and visionary Ray Bradbury (1920-): "The best scientist is open to experience and begins with romance — the idea that anything is possible."

So what's an open-minded skeptic? Obviously, it's someone

who doesn't go hog-wild with ghost fantasies every time there's a strange noise in the house. But it's also one who takes dear old Aristotle at his word. This pivotal Greek philosopher (384-322 B.C. – or B.C.E. for the politically correct) said that we all start life with minds that are *tabulae rasae*, "empty slates." And we use the best tools we have — our powers of observation — to "write" on those slates.

Open-minded skeptics must be objective thinkers, people who not only can keep a mass of facts between their ears, but who can see, analyze, interpret, judge, deduce, imagine, and be wide open to better information as it comes in – *and* be prepared to change their opinions when it does. A pretty tall order, since none of us can be absolutely without bias. As the German philosopher Friedrich Nietzsche (1844-1900) said, "Convictions are more dangerous foes of truth than lies."

What's more, if observation is going to be the tool that moves us toward our answers, it has to be a chorus, not a solo. We must consider the totality of human observation throughout history, not just the observations of ourselves or those who think the way we do.

Zero

How much can we – believer or skeptic – really *know*?

The celebrated French philosopher Rene Descartes (1596-1650) started from scratch with the proposition *"Je pense, donc je suis."* ("I think, therefore I am.") He built his philosophy and mathematics from there. But toward the end of his life, as with many great thinkers, he began to realize that all thought, all philosophy, all mathematics, all perception.... It all ends in silence. In the end, he realized, even *"Je pense, donc je suis"* isn't enough. When all is said and done, what we really know about our universe, our world, our minds, ourselves is zip, zero, *nada*.

So we turn to religion for our knowledge, right?

Not so fast.

On this planet are religions of every description and, as we will see, their clergy and followers don't always agree on what these religions believe. The "Big Three," however, are Judaism, Christianity and Muhammedanism. These are "people of the book," so to speak. Jews, Christians and Muslims base their beliefs and practices on their holy scriptures. But because clergy and scholars often disagree on the meaning of this or that passage in the Torah, the Bible or the Qur'an, life for the ordinary believer can get complicated. All three religions are split into many different sects precisely because neither their leaders nor members can agree on exactly what to believe or how to believe it.

There's another critical issue with scriptures that's seldom mentioned. The earliest known religious symbols, and the writings of the earliest known civilizations, literally were carved in stone. The Torah, the Bible and the Qur'an, however, were passed down in manuscript form – hand copy after hand copy after hand copy. Even the Qur'an, the youngest of the "Big Three" holy books, appeared some nine centuries before Johannes Gutenberg (1400-1468) trotted out the first printing press.

The people who did the laborious job of copying the scriptures were called scribes, and they worked in a time when only society's elite could read and write. In the ancient world, however, many scribes were barely literate themselves. We have many ancient scripture manuscripts that have serious discrepancies, careless mistakes and even deliberate errors. There are even some with marginal notes by scribes condemning other scribes for changing the text.

In the centuries between the beginning of Christianity and the advent of the printing press, the Christian Church in particular rocked with theological disputes. Is Jesus Christ truly God? Is Jesus Christ truly man? Should Christians marry and have children, or should they just wait for Jesus's promised return? Should icons or statues be allowed in churches? Does the bread and wine actually become the body and blood of Christ at the liturgy? What are the proper dates and ways to celebrate Christmas and Easter? What place, if any, should the Virgin Mary have in the spiritual life of Christians? What's the role of the clergy? Should there even be clergy? Should Jews be forced to become Christians? Should witches be burned? ...and so on and so on to the point of absolute madness. During the second and third centuries, some Christians even debated whether there was one God or two – one good and one evil.

By the 5th century, scribes had become a respected and educated professional class. But their education meant that they had their own opinions during the great theological debates of that period. Some are known to have made deliberate changes in Bible manuscripts here and there to favor their own points of view.

The fact is that, while we may believe that the Torah or the Bible or the Qur'an are the Word of God, we have no certainty about what the original written words of the authors, whether they be Moses or the evangelists or the Prophet, actually were.

So when it comes to certain knowledge of anything through either science or religion – there really isn't any. It's all – *all* – a matter of faith. Many "clergy" of science or religion are just too scared or too pigheaded to admit it.

In the early 21st century there is hope, however, because segments of the scientific and maybe even religious clergy are opening up at last. Quantum physics, the unfolding wonders of the human mind, a growing appreciation for non-western points of view, the discrediting of "matter is all there is to the universe" as the basis of science, "New Age" thinking, and even a budding acceptance by mainstream science and medicine of the value of spirituality – all are contributing to the gradual re-enchantment of reality and a greater curiosity about the paranormal.

Is it much of a step from there to the insight that the paranormal is a real factor – maybe the prime factor — in human existence? Can we now realize what it means that every culture in the history of the planet has experienced – even been centered on – the paranormal?

More and more mainstream scientists privately admit that we must look "outside the box" if we hope to understand reality at all, never mind the paranormal. With what I've seen of the paranormal, the "box" isn't even in the same building: I believe that accepting and understanding the paranormal is the key to all science, religion and knowledge.

The one message that invisible oxcart driver at *Bara Hack* seemed to carry for me was: "It's the first day of school, kid."

Whether you realize it or not, you had a "first day of school" too, and it wasn't at kindergarten in your old home town. It might have been as you cried after your mother's funeral, and she touched you on the shoulder. Maybe it was the "angel" who prompted you to wait an extra second before stepping off that curb – into the path of the bus you hadn't seen. Perhaps it was the first time you heard footsteps in the attic, and knew there was nobody there. It could have been the day you put down that toy or piece of clothing, only to look back a moment later to find it gone. Maybe it was that dream you never forgot, or a near-death experience that changed you forever.

The encounter might have been beautiful. It might have been horrifying. But it started to teach you. And there have been more hints, clues and lessons – many more – whether you have heeded them or not, probably every day of your life. These might have been nothing more than feelings – feelings of presences, feelings that there was something more than met the eye, even feelings that you didn't quite belong where you were or where you are.

Maybe, like our scientists, you have asked questions that spurred only more questions. But there are answers, I assure you. There are things we can know, not just with our minds but with our hearts.

Welcome to the first day of school.

2

From Square One

O small beginnings, ye are great and strong,
Based on a faithful heart and weariless brain!
Ye build the future fair, ye conquer wrong,
Ye earn the crown, and wear it not in vain.
-James Russell Lowell, *American Poet*

Since we can't rely on either science or religion for all our answers, we're on our own with our little *tabulae rasae*. Perhaps by sharing some of my own strange odyssey into the paranormal, I can give us a few starting sentences for our "empty slates."

I've always been a ferocious questioner, as I hope you are. My experiences at *Bara Hack* in 1971 only made me more so. America today seems awash with ghost hunters, but in my early days it wasn't considered a normal activity for anyone but occultists. As a matter of fact it wouldn't even have occurred to most people, whether they were questioners or not. I think there was just as much paranormal activity then as now, but people tended not to talk about it for fear of ridicule. Even today, the first question I usually get in a case is, "Do you think we're crazy?"

There were a few serious researchers then, including four or five first-generation greats. These included philosopher and parapsychologist Brian Riley (1927-) of the University of London, whom I knew fairly well in my salad days, and prolific author, ghost hunter and parapsychologist Hans Holzer (1920-). In 1975, Dr. Riley, who actually visited *Bara Hack* after my group finished there, authored an outstanding course in parapsychology, *The Psi Effect*. "Psi" (pronounced "p-see") is a Greek letter that's used as a shorthand term for psychic phenomena.

Today there are many more good researchers, both inside and outside the academic world, but there have always been far more frauds, hoaxers and quick-buck artists, and they do the field terrible harm.

Aside from the latter, there were and are three kinds of people who investigate the paranormal, and all usually do so because they've had a weird experience of one kind or another, and they're curious about whether it was real.

There are the trained parapsychologists like White, Riley and Holzer. These usually are psychiatrists, philosophers, religion experts, medical doctors or psychologists who do postgraduate work at one of the few institutions that offer formal studies in this realm or, in the old days, studies that amounted to it. Often they serve on university faculties. They do some field work, but spend much time in the laboratory, trying to study psychic phenomena of one type or another.

The second group has always consisted of people like me: Those with degree work in fields that can be related to the paranormal (philosophy, theology and psychology, in my case) who go out and do "seat of the pants" field research, and perhaps contribute to the literature on the subject. Often they're in professions, such as medicine, religion or even journalism, that allow them to make paranormal research a part of their work.

The third, and by far the largest, group consists of amateurs or curiosity seekers who spend their weekends camped out at cemeteries, abandoned prisons or spooky houses, trying to have and record paranormal experiences. They're often loaded down with high-tech gear like electromagnetic field (EMF) meters, infrared thermal scanners and ion detectors they seldom understand fully, and that really don't mean much in the end. These folks get most of the media attention.

This group has sparked a growing industry: paranormal tourism, which attracts hordes of people to everything from "ghost walks" in old city neighborhoods to lengthy excursions and conventions at the Gettysburg Civil War battlefield and many other historic high spots.

I don't mean to impugn all those in the third group, though some of its members can and do wreak plenty of havoc in cases they have no business dealing with. The group does include many fine, intelligent and sincere seekers after truth – many "ferocious questioners" — and there's nothing wrong with that.

Seminary Ghost Hunters?

Your first question to me might be why six students for the Roman Catholic priesthood were out in the woods of *Bara Hack* in 1971 hunting ghosts in the first place. After all, the Roman Catholic Church has always been very edgy about the concept of ghosts, has no specific doctrine on the subject, and (officially, at least) is absolutely unshakable in its condemnation of psychics, mediums, and any attempts to communicate with the dead.

As a serious Roman Catholic in my salad days, I had a theory about something that was an embarrassment to trendy Catholic intellectuals by the 1970s: purgatory. This is an idea that some claim has been around since the beginning of Christianity, but it was only developed as a doctrine in the Middle Ages. Purgatory is supposedly a place or state in which departed souls not quite bad enough for hell have to stay for an indefinite period of suffering. There they are "purged" (hence the word "purgatory") of their sins until they are pure enough to enter heaven. People on Earth are said to be able to help souls in purgatory along by praying for them.

Having an interest in ghosts already, I wondered if the "earthbound spirits" or "tortured souls" known to every culture in history might in fact be souls in purgatory. In fact I felt sorry for them. And I talked five other seminarians and the photo guy into coming along as witnesses, just in case something actually happened! *Bara Hack* was to be my first laboratory for testing the theory, but the questions my experiences shook out of me led in a direction that had nothing to do with purgatory.

For example, our phantom oxcart driver showed not the least sign of being dead at all, never mind suffering in purgatory. He seemed to be going about his everyday business in a world that had nothing to do with ours. So did the invisible children we heard, laughing up and down the brook the first evening we spent at *Bara Hack*. So did the group of invisible men, talking in low voices near the old village cemetery in the dark of a moonless night. So did the bluish, wispy figures moving among the trees at dusk. So did the various dads, moms, cows, dogs and farm implements we heard, but couldn't see, at any given moment at this Village of Voices.

"Are these really the souls of dead people?" I asked myself. "Are there 'ghosts' of oxcarts and farm tools? Without our bodies, are we still fully us?" And most importantly, "Could these ghost experiences – and those of millions of other people throughout history and folklore – have more to do with *time* than with death?"

Despite the "skepticemics," paranormal experiences (especially ghosts) pervade human history and folklore. But, like most children of the arrogant 20th century, I assumed that previous generations lived on generous helpings of naiveté, backward science, lousy theology, and even stupidity.

In doing field research, meanwhile, I realized from the get-go that a number of hurdles had to be cleared before concluding that something paranormal was going on in a given case. People hearing voices and seeing things when nobody else was could be more schizophrenic than haunted. That would-be poltergeist could be mice or ground squirrels in the house. That bruise on the child's back more likely came from an abusive parent than from a spirit. And there were always mistakes, hoaxes, and just plain imagination.

As a seminary student, of course, I was preconditioned to believe in Satan and demons. These, I assumed, were responsible for many – even most – ghost experiences that weren't the result of "natural" causes. The ones that weren't demonic, I thought, might fit my purgatory hypothesis. At least that was my opinion before I started tangling with real ghosts.

There were plenty of those during the *Bara Hack* investigation and in the years immediately following. Among the latter were the bizarre incident of the weeping Indian ghost (West Springfield, Massachusetts, 1972), the strange case of the disturbed grave (New Britain, Connecticut, 1973), the farmhouse haunted by something that liked to turn on lights (Coventry, Connecticut, 1973), the singular affair of the ghost in the checkered shirt (Montreal, Quebec, 1975); the peculiar phenomenon of the phantom deer (Cortland, New York, 1976); and, of course, the terrifying poltergeist outbreaks in Bridgeport (1974) and New Haven, Connecticut (1978), both recounted in my previous books *Faces at the Window: First Hand Accounts of the Paranormal in Southern New England* (1998) and *Footsteps in the Attic: More First Hand Accounts of the Paranormal in New England* (2002), respectively.

By the mid-1970s, though, my church superiors were scowling down upon me with folded arms because of my paranormal research. People think that clergy in general, and Roman Catholic priests in particular, are trained to deal with the paranormal in case they're called upon to perform exorcisms. That isn't true. Most Roman Catholic dioceses (regional groups of parishes and institutions headed by a bishop) have one hand-picked priest who does hush-hush studies of the paranormal, or at least "demonology," and relevant areas of psychology. Most parish priests know little or nothing about the paranormal and, if a case should arise and they can actually be convinced that it's genuine, will refer it to the diocese. You never hear about this because an institution as ancient as the Roman Church is very good at keeping its secrets.

The same ignorance about the paranormal is common among clergy of other religions, where preconceived notions, confusion, denial and small thinking often are the rule. There are always shining exceptions, but I can think of no one who can make a bigger pig's breakfast out of a paranormal investigation than a typical member of the clergy.

When it came to my own paranormal work, the scowlers included the man who was essentially my boss, Bishop John A. Marshall of the Diocese of Burlington, Vermont, where I would have served if ordained to the priesthood. "Rid yourself of this obsession!" His Excellency spat in a 1975 letter to me. Were it not for the fact that my older brother, Bob, was a prominent priest and theologian with a string of academic and ecclesiastical honors after his name, I think the good prelate would have gotten rid of me then and there.

Neither the bishop nor my seminary superiors knew the half of it. Since my first encounters at *Bara Hack*, I had noticed what anyone else would have called psychic, or at least intuitive, abilities. While I went through my initial "Is this really paranormal?" procedures (and still do) in every case, I always knew when a ghost was around and just where it was. On some occasions, I would even know *who* it was. What confused me was that some ghosts seemed non-human but not demonic, and many "felt" like different "species," even from each other. Those impressions helped nudge me toward the unusual theories and methods I use today.

Open-minded as I was trying to be, I found all this very disturbing because it didn't correlate with my religious beliefs. I didn't *want* to be psychic! I *wanted* ghosts to be dead people or demons! And where the hell was purgatory? I was on thin ice as it was, but had my superiors gotten a whiff of anything psychic or mediumistic from me, I would have been out the door like a shot, Bob or no Bob! So I clammed up about these budding abilities, even when accompanied on cases by other seminarians, friends or even fellow investigators.

My few friends in the "psychic community" sometimes called me on it, like longtime investigator and medium Lorraine Warren (1927-). "You're very psychic, but you block it!" Lorraine would say. "You could really help people if you would just use it." But I smothered these abilities and tried to soldier on with paranormal research for its own sake. It wouldn't be until the end of the 20th century that I would start to psychically "come out of the closet."

I was learning more about photography, which I've always relied on for evidence in my cases. I say "evidence," not "proof." From the beginning, when odd streaks and figures (known to ghost hunters as "extras") appeared in our *Bara Hack* photographs, I knew enough to have the negatives examined by experts. In that early period, they were checked by folks at MK Photo Lab of East Hartford, Connecticut, my native town. Even in that pre-digital era, before personal computers and sophisticated photo-processing software, an expert could pretty much tell if something on a negative was a reflection, lens flare, a stuck shutter or any number of other glitches.

They couldn't proclaim, "there's a ghost in that picture!" but by eliminating all the known hiccups, they could say that this streak, face or figure was "an anomaly." Eventually I would learn photography professionally as a journalist and (as I joke with my American audiences) at taxpayers' expense in the U.S. Coast Guard Reserve. But to this day I still use experts to examine any picture I believe has anomalies.

In the meantime, back in the mid-1970s, all was turmoil for me. So I was relieved to find a few sympathetic faculty members at the seminary where I got my philosophy degree, Wadhams Hall, in Ogdensburg, New York, in 1975. Fr. Robert McGinnis there arranged a private course for me in abnormal psychology, so I could better judge what sort of people I was dealing with in ghost cases. I was able to do some very eye-opening field work at the nearby Ogdensburg State Hospital and, later, at Norwich State Hospital, in Connecticut, all in times when psychiatric inpatients were far more common than they are today. I was to continue these studies in graduate school.

It was at these two psychiatric hospitals that my quest to keep an open mind really got a workout. There were a few isolated cases that could be called demonic possession. And I witnessed paranormal phenomena in the presence of hospital staff on several occasions.

More very uncomfortable questions started to occur to me.

Ever look into the eyes of a schizophrenic? It can be unnerving in a gut-wrenching way, given the knowing, deeply sane look one sometimes gets in return. When patients reported paranormal happenings, including alternate states of consciousness or experiences of other realities (and when drugs weren't a factor), psychotherapists I knew often would suspect not just schizophrenia but temporal lobe epilepsy or schizotypal personality disorder.

Was it possible that psychiatric or neural conditions such as these didn't *cause* imaginary paranormal experiences, but created conditions in the brain *to open doors to real ones*? Later I would even wonder if people suffering from dissociative identity disorder (multiple personalities) were actually in touch with real lives they were living simultaneously – quite possible under some interpretations of quantum physics.

While I was studying abnormal psychology, I heard about the work of the eminent medical researchers Frank Brown of Northwestern University in Evanston, Illinois, and Rutger Wever of the Max Planck Institute in Munich, West Germany. While hospital staffers I knew would joke about psychiatric patients being harder to handle when the moon was full, scientists like Drs. Brown and Wever were proving the connection between the Earth's magnetic field (influenced, of course, by the moon and sun) and the behaviors of living systems, including humans. It was found that the weak DC (direct-current) electrical fields around our own bodies can interact dramatically with the other fields around us, which do much to determine our bodily cycles.

Much of this, of course, was heresy to mainstream psychiatry at the time.

Out on My Ear

Bishops and shrinks weren't the only ones who didn't appreciate my outlandish questions or the opinions they generated. By the end of 1975 I was in graduate theological studies at St. Vladimir Seminary near New York City, and faculty members there were much less tolerant than the ones at Wadhams Hall. It was at "St. Vlad's," in 1977, only two or three years before I would have been ordained to the priesthood, that I had my final showdown with church authorities over my paranormal work. Based on an utterly ludicrous accusation that I had "performed an exorcism on a fellow student," I was at last given my *congé* without so much as a hearing.

So much for the priesthood. It was out the window along with purgatory. Everything I had worked and studied so hard for was down the pipe because of a false accusation, and it was small consolation that I finally had freedom to pursue my paranormal research as I wished — or so I thought.

If anything, I'm a survivor. By late 1977 I had dusted myself off and was enrolled in the Master of Liberal Arts Program at Trinity College in Hartford, Connecticut, where I continued graduate work in philosophy, psychology and several other fields. With my newfound freedom of speech, I wrote my first books. These were two modest little tomes entitled *The Occult* (1977) and *The Psychical Research Team Counseling Handbook: Preventive Medicine for the Occult* (1979), both published by a Chicago firm and now mercifully out of print.

In case you're wondering, the Psychical Research Team of New England was a little group I ran for a few years in that decade. It included some fellow seminarians, but also such early luminaries as Dr. Riley, Ed and Lorraine Warren, and Fr. William Charbonneau (a Roman Catholic priest who somehow got away with being a paranormal investigator, though a very low-key one). But that was before I realized that it's best to work solo, or with a few picked professionals, in order to avoid the little feuds and intrigues that are life's primary pleasure for so many people who join things.

'The Haunter' and 'The Children in the Corner'

My paranormal experiences thus far had shaken me up, but the shockers just kept on coming. I was about to be hit right between the eyes by two cases I've rarely seen the like of since.

By October 1978 I was living in a lakeside cottage in Tolland, Connecticut, and barely supporting myself by writing on grant money for, of all things, the Connecticut Dance Theater. The case of "The Haunter" of York Harbor, Maine, fully recounted in *Footsteps in the Attic: More First-Hand Accounts of the Paranormal in New England*, began with a phone call one afternoon that month. It was from the older sister of the young girl at the center of the case – a young girl who was at the same time a live-and-kicking student at the University of Connecticut *and* a ghost haunting a house in the Maine seaside town, some 125 miles away.

By dumb luck or subconscious design the weekend before the phone call, both sisters and some friends had been driving through southern Maine, and they happened to pass the very house. In complete shock, the young girl recognized the place from vivid dreams, though she had never been there before, and she ran to the door. The couple there froze with terror at first sight of the kid, swearing that she was the ghost haunting their home!

The petrified couple swore to me in lengthy conversations later that they had seen the girl *in transparent form* doing everything the girl told me she had dreamt of doing in the house.

What had we here? A demon? Nope. A departed spirit? Forget it.

Only a few months after the Maine mystery came another that was nearly as bizarre.

I traveled a great deal in early 1979, finding myself in Ottawa, Ontario, Canada, at one point. One of my associates there, an officer in the Canadian army, knew about my paranormal proclivities. He put me in touch with some local relatives of his who had confided in him about a very unusual happening. I visited the home, in a relatively new, upper-crust subdivision just outside Canada's capital city. I already had the habit of checking each room of a house before allowing anyone to tell me what was going on. In doing this, I told myself and others that I was relying on my experience of "knowing what to look for." That was true, but I also was giving a grudging nod to my psychic abilities. Most of the house "felt" fine, but it was in the basement that I got the faint but clear impression of two children. The only way to describe the confusing feeling: They were there, but they were far away.

Usually I would have heard the family's story before telling them my impressions, to avoid suggestibility, but I knew I could verify their tale with my army friend, who had heard it before I even got involved. So, planted at the kitchen table with Mom and Dad (their only child, a boy of ten, was at school), I told them I had gotten the impression of two children in the basement. The blood drained from their faces, and they simply stared at each other. The hair stood up on the back of even my neck! Here's the story I heard:

"On a Saturday morning last month, I sent our son, Alex, down to the basement to get something," the jumpy, thirty-ish father explained. "He ran back up the stairs and shouted for my wife and me to come down and 'see the kids.' He looked terrified."

"Alex has a real imagination," Mom chimed in, casting a nervous glance at Dad.

Dad trotted downstairs, but he saw nothing in the corner Alex indicated. Neither did Alex.

"They were just there!" the boy cried. Then the two of them searched the basement, looking behind boxes and checking under the stairs. Dad inspected the windows and the hatchway to the back yard. All was secure. "I'm telling you, Dad, there were two kids here!" Alex cried. Dad could see that he was sincere.

This happened again the following Saturday. But this time it was to be a Saturday the entire family would never forget.

"Dad, they're back! They're back!" Alex cried from the top of the basement stairs.

"Alex, there's no way anybody could get in down there!" Dad replied, irritated. He exchanged disgusted glances with his wife as all three clumped down the stairs and stood on the concrete floor.

At first, nothing looked different. Then...

"There!" Alex pointed toward the northeast corner. "The kids" were there alright. Dad froze where he stood. He could hear his wife's sharp intake of breath before she covered her mouth to block a scream.

Huddled in the corner were a boy, who looked about eight years old, and a girl who seemed a few years younger. They had their arms around each other, but the whole scene was "abnormal," Dad said.

"There was this eerie kind of darkness surrounding them, and both kids kind of shimmered a little. My God, it was unbelievable!" Dad recalled. "Both had short, dark hair, and they were dressed very strangely. Both had on what looked like dark blue, one-piece jumpsuits, like something you'd go jogging or sky-diving in."

Mom piped up, "They looked frightened, and at first they didn't seem to see us." She was shaking as she spoke.

These other-worldly children suddenly seemed to notice the family.

"They looked terrified, and the girl started to cry. But the weirdest thing about it was that we couldn't hear a thing!" Mom recalled. "By this time, Alex was clinging to me and shaking."

When I asked about the temperature and general feeling in the basement during the encounter, they both said their "skin was crawling" so badly that they never noticed the temperature. Rooms supposedly get cold when ghosts are present, something I've experienced in very few cases, strangely enough.

The worst part of the incident, the couple agreed, was when the children started crying out to them. Again, they could see the mouths moving and the fear in the children's eyes as they continued to cling to one another, but the family could hear nothing.

Then, without warning, the scene changed.

"It was like a flash of black, then everything was back to normal. The two kids were gone – just like that!"

According to the couple, nearly a month had gone by, and there had been no repeat performance. Of course, Alex refused to descend those stairs again, and they were thinking of selling the house. I tried to discuss the history of the place, but there was none: My new friends were the first owners, and the subdivision site had previously been part of the great north woods from time immemorial.

"Who were those poor children?" Mom pleaded. "What can we do for them if they come back?"

I had no idea how to answer either question. "Just pray for them," was the only answer I could give.

After eight years of paranormal investigation, I felt I knew less than when I'd started. The York Harbor and Ottawa cases left me feeling powerless.

Here's what I knew:

• The classical idea of ghosts and what to do about them couldn't come close to explaining what I was seeing. In fact, the deeper I looked into most of my cases, the less they were what they appeared to be.

• What I still referred to as "demons" didn't seem to have the same theology as I – or anyone else – did. I was becoming very uncertain about the true nature and intentions of these non-human creatures.

• I never used Ouija boards and séances, but when they had been used in a case before I got there, they only made things worse. And when people were involved in the occult at all, it tended to attract "demons."

• I have never been a medium, but if an entity did manage to communicate with me (usually through someone else), I found I could seldom trust what it said.

• In cases I felt were demonic, clergy, holy water, prayers and the like from any religion didn't always work. If they did work, it usually wasn't for long.

• The only actual evidence I could find of death was at funerals.

Here's what I suspected:

• Traditional explanations for ghosts – and probably for all things paranormal — were pitifully inadequate. If there was to be an answer at all, it would have to come from a combination of many, perhaps all, sciences, religions and philosophies: from the totality of human experience.

• In every case I investigated, the people involved, and what was happening in their lives, seemed to have as much to do with the phenomena as any ghost did, sometimes more so.

• Entirely new theories and methods were needed.

• There was much, much more to the paranormal than I had ever thought possible, and there were far too few qualified scientists, philosophers and theologians studying the subject, mostly because they didn't take it seriously or were afraid of ridicule.

Finding Schroedinger's Cat

My personal breakthrough finally came in 1979, just after the Ottawa case. It took the form of a book called: *The Tao of Physics: An Exploration of the Parallels Between Modern Physics and Eastern Mysticism* by professor, physicist and mystic Fritjof Capra. It was published in 1975 and I'd had it since 1978, but hadn't had a chance to read it.

The first statement that jumped out at me was:

"Physicists do not need mysticism, and mystics do not need physics, but humanity needs both."

I was excited! Here was someone combining the ancient with the modern, bringing together many disciplines to come up with a more complete vision of reality and how it actually worked! Specifically, Capra talked about the wild, and wildly complex, world of quantum physics as a key to understanding reality, a key that we had only just discovered, but that was somehow known to the ancients, especially in India and China.

I certainly had experience with spirituality and mysticism, and I had studied Eastern philosophy and religion. I had even studied physics in the normal course of my schooling. *The Journal of the American Society for Psychical Research* had contained some hints that parapsychologists were starting to notice quantum physics. But reading Capra, something "clicked," and I believed I had found some new approaches that truly might lead to understanding the paranormal.

After Capra came *Taking the Quantum Leap* by Fred Alan Wolf (1981) *Quantum Reality: Beyond the New Physics* by Nick Herbert (1985), *The Self-Aware Universe* by Amit Goswami (1993), and many more.

By 1980 I had fallen head-over-heels in love with quantum probabilities, fractals, concepts of molecular consciousness, Schroedinger's cat (a thought experiment about people making reality real), resonances, the Alain Aspect Experiment, quantum electrodynamics and, most of all, the multiple worlds interpretation (MWI) of quantum physics, originated by Hugh Everett (1930-1982) of Princeton University.

When we think of "other worlds," we've been conditioned by mainstream science, and certainly by science fiction, to think of other planets. But the MWI gives us infinite numbers of worlds infinitely farther away *and* no farther away than the ends of our psychic fingertips. We can call them "parallel" or "simultaneous" worlds and universes, or perhaps "other dimensions."

Physicists who accept the MWI interpret it in several ways,

but I quickly became convinced that it was the key to what I was scratching my head over in paranormal research. The MWI theorizes that these parallel worlds are something like soap bubbles in a bathtub. They move over, under, around and through one another. The walls or membranes of certain bubbles intersect at this or that place. Two or more bubbles may be attached for a period of time.

If that's not complicated enough, here's where it gets worse. Somewhere within all the worlds, everything that is even remotely possible, past or future, already exists. Take two of these "bubble" worlds, and the only difference may be that in one you are twenty-five years old and living in Bolivia, and in the other you died 30,000 years ago in a UFO crash in a country that never existed in the "bubble" in which you're reading this book. Take another "bubble," and it *still is* 30,000 years ago, and you never existed at all! Take another two universes and they may be so alien that you would recognize nothing, including the critters that live there.

Just as with bubbles in the bathtub, parallel worlds constantly interact. In some interpretations of the MWI, new worlds are being created by the gazillions at every moment — by chance or by choices that we – and any other intelligent "observer" out there — make. Drop a coffee cup while washing the dishes tomorrow, and you will very literally create (or more accurately, "make real") another "bubble" universe, which will split off from the one in which you *didn't* drop the coffee cup.

I subscribe to an interpretation that's a little different. I believe that the two "bubbles" – the one with the broken cup and the one where the cup made it – already exist, and have existed since the Creation. In the nanosecond before the cup heads for the floor, your mind's own psychic power connects (subconsciously, by chance or design, as it does all day long) *with you* in other "bubble" worlds – in this case, the one in which the cup breaks.

Analogy: The Multiverse

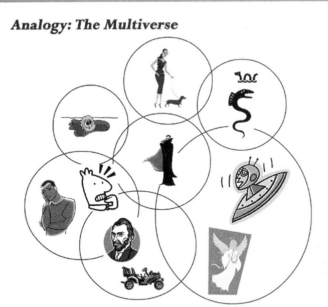

The author's conception of the quantum "multiverse." Though overly simple and very crude, it conveys the basic idea. The "bubbles" represent worlds (actually constituting whole universes) that exist simultaneously, in accord with some understandings of the multiple worlds interpretation of quantum physics. Somewhere in this multiversal system, anything that can possibly exist already exists. People who are dead in our world are alive in every stage of their lives in other worlds. There are many worlds in which we ourselves are dead. In some it is our past, while in others it is our future. Some are completely alien, with scenery and life we wouldn't recognize. Where these "bubbles" overlap or blend, the denizens of each can interact. The author believes this can explain not only ghosts but UFOs, out-of-place creatures and other paranormal phenomena.

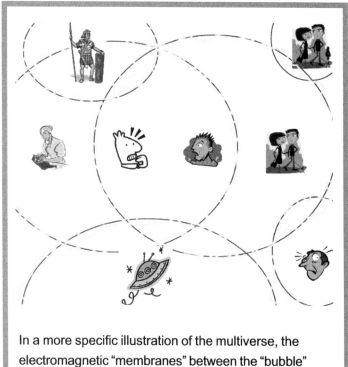

In a more specific illustration of the multiverse, the electromagnetic "membranes" between the "bubble" worlds are seen. The author believes that he has actual photographs of these "world boundaries." At the top right of the illustration, note the same couple "walking" something. In one world it could be a dog. In the other, it could be a kangaroo.

That causes both "bubble" worlds to combine, and you're minus one coffee cup. Your conscious mind keeps humming along in one "bubble" world or the other, we're not sure which. But since this sort of thing happens with every choice or happenstance in our lives, what's one "bubble" here and there? We move through tens of thousands or more every day!

Your conscious mind is right here, right now. Your subconscious mind consists of the zillions of other "yous" in zillions of other "bubble" worlds.

By the way, if you hadn't psychically connected with yourself *enough* in the cup-cracking world, you wouldn't have brought the worlds together. They might just have brushed past each other. You might just have heard a cup break at your feet. You would have had a brief paranormal experience!

This may seem impossibly complicated, not to mention absolutely nuts. Physicists don't even understand it, even though the math and the experiments say it. But read on. It'll grow on you.

Remember the old "time paradox" on which Hollywood has based so many cheesy movies? Somebody goes back in time and shoots her own great-grandfather, so how can she ever be born? In this infinite mass of "bubble" worlds, there's no problem. Whacking the ancestor merely brings into conscious reality another world in which the guy is dead. The one you have your conscious roots in doesn't change at all, and you keep humming along as always.

Welcome to quantum reality!

Forget the universe; from now on we're living in the "multiverse"! And the multiverse's most prominent signpost is the paranormal; our "iceberg" gets bigger and bigger.

That phantom oxcart driver at *Bara Hack* may have been dead in our little world, but he wasn't dead at all in thousands, perhaps millions, of parallel, simultaneous worlds in the multiverse. He was going about his day in millions of these, and the seven of us happened to be in the right place at the right time – right at the conjunction of two world boundaries or "membranes," as physicists sometimes say — to hear him in one of them.

And it's a big multiverse. It occurred to me that what I had considered demons — the non-human critters I was "feeling" in many cases, especially poltergeists — could in fact be entities from parallel worlds very unlike our own.

Those "psychos" in the state hospitals I'd studied in? Perhaps at least some of them just had wider consciousness than the rest of us: Their conscious minds embraced their own existence in more than one world. Some worlds they lived in were beautiful, some were hideous, some were both. So-called primitive people, who were aware of all these realities, would have considered these people holy. We considered them bonkers.

Psychics and mediums? As much as I hated to admit it, quantum reality could legitimize them, too. They were highly sensitive people who thought they were in touch with a "spirit world" beyond some "veil." In fact, no matter how goofy, sappy or retrograde their interpretations, they were quite literally in touch with other vibrant worlds and people – living people who were dead here.

Our living ghost in Maine? Probably a mutual experience of the same parallel worlds by three different people. Those unfortunate children in Canada? Likely a brief conjunction of parallel worlds – close enough to cause mutual perception and mutual terror. And what did this mean for the rest of us? At the very least, like that UCONN student, it meant that *we* could be ghosts to those in worlds where it was elsewhere and elsewhen. To them, *we* would be in a "spirit world"!

These zany concepts flew against everything I had been taught to think about the universe, about time, about ourselves as individuals, and certainly about ghosts. But I found that once I started to get my mind around these quantum ideas, they made a frightening amount of sense.

Of course, harmonizing the paranormal with the "new physics" wasn't my idea. As I've said, several far more academically qualified people than I in the ASPR (to which I belonged then and now) and the Parapsychological Association were doing the same thing – and are still working at it. But, with the exception of a few "disciples" of my last two books, I believe

I'm the only in-the-field ghost hunter who applies multiverse concepts to every case.

In the 1980s, however, I quickly found that most physicists weren't wild about the idea, often because interpretations of quantum physics vary so much. By the middle of that decade I had hunted down and buttonholed a number of physicists, mostly on college campuses. When I told them I was trying to bring together paranormal research and quantum physics, some thought I was just plain nuts. Others pronounced, "You have the wrong academic degrees" or words to that effect. Still others were intrigued. A few even seemed to know what I was talking about. But all begged off on my invitations to join me on a case or two to see for themselves. Most had an unbecoming, but understandable, attitude that ran something like, "I'm a physicist, and you don't even have a doctorate. Know your place!"

At various points over the decades, my investigatory "gang" has included two parapsychologists, a psychiatric social worker, several hand-picked clergy, a soil engineer, an expert in death and dying, three professional photography experts, an electrical engineer, a handful of other paranormal investigators, several professed skeptics, and a medical doctor. All have managed to get past my academic shortcomings in favor of my long experience. As I write this in 2005, however, I have yet to find a physicist willing to stick his or her academic neck out by joining me on even one investigation.

I had and still have something none of these reluctant physicists do: Decades "in the trenches," seeing what can only be quantum reality in action in people's everyday lives in its most magnificent and dramatic form – the paranormal.

As this new day was dawning for me in paranormal research, I came to yet another realization: The ghosts, quantum or not, weren't about to pay me. The gods, however, seemed determined to make me a writer. I was pretty good at it, had done some part-time work for three weekly newspapers, and had published a few articles and my two little books. By mid-1979 I had moved to Rhode Island to take a reporter's job at the only newspaper in New England whose editor would talk to me: *The Pawtuxet Valley Daily Times* (today the *Kent County Daily Times*).

I was to have a long and rewarding career as a journalist in America's tiniest state. Only forty-eight miles long and thirty-seven miles wide, Rhode Island is a closely-knit little place where people tend to know each other, and where anything can and does happen. I would even win three awards for journalism and writing, and I would end up as a news editor at one of New England's largest daily newspapers, the *Providence Journal-Bulletin*.

As far as paranormal research was concerned, I quickly learned that there was good news and bad news. The good news: I finally was getting paid – rather than sacked — for asking tough questions (albeit mostly about politics). The bad news: I *still* had to keep my trap shut about being a ghost hunter; that information would not have done wonders for my credibility as a local newsman.

Nevertheless, I ghost-chased with gusto if not publicity. I found a number of new cases in my adopted state and nearby Massachusetts. And I developed new theories and methods around what I knew – theology, philosophy, and a little bit of the psychic. When I wrapped them all in this revolutionary, multiverse point of view, successes resulted where before there had been only frustration. For the first time, I was genuinely able to start helping people caught up in these frightening events, mainly by teaching them what it really was they were experiencing. I found that understanding had an amazing way of banishing the fear and enabling people to take control of their own situations.

Quantum physics wasn't all I had fallen in love with by the

early 1980s. Since leaving the seminary it had dawned on me that a new life loomed mysteriously ahead, and that marriage and family were now among the quantum probabilities. My fondest prayer was for a wife who would love God, love our children and love me, in that order. And it wasn't long before that prayer was answered.

In 1981 I married my wonderful and endlessly understanding wife, Jackie, who surely must be a direct descendant of that patient Old Testament forefather, Job. I knew from the beginning that my bride was very sensitive, intuitive and extremely psychic. She had had some frightening paranormal experiences of her own, and for the first sixteen years or so of our marriage, she didn't participate in any of my cases. We rarely even discussed them. As it was, Jackie had her hands full trying to domesticate a certain old bachelor, not to mention mothering two sons who were all too much like their dad!

Still, Jackie sometimes dropped hints and shared feelings that really helped in my cases. Since 1998 she has become a little more involved, and has been a tremendous teammate because she often sees things I don't see, and points out possibilities that I miss. It was Jackie who helped me understand that, in dealing with frightened people, it can't be all theory. It has to be personal and compassionate. Understanding, seasoned with compassion, is even better than explanations when it comes to banishing fear.

Turning on the Lights

Despite this progress into the mid 1980s, paranormal *Nirvana* remained out of reach because new and nagging questions arose:

• The multiverse approach certainly worked when I encountered ghosts and "demons." But what about when I *didn't* encounter them? With all these bubble-like worlds constantly sloshing through one another, why wasn't the whole planet awash in blatant paranormal phenomena "24/7"?

• Why would one distressed family attract and "feed" a "demon" or poltergeist when twenty others in the same circumstances didn't?

• What triggered overt paranormal phenomena? What was I missing?

The logical approach was to break down each case I judged to be paranormal and see what it had in common with others. One of the first common characteristics was what I always felt in the presence of paranormal entities, whether ghosts, "demons," or what I was starting to think were the boundaries or membranes of different worlds at sites of paranormal disturbances. It varied depending on the place, the entity and the kind of entity, but it was always an electrical tingle on my skin – sometimes gentle, sometimes a real shock.

Electromagnetism! Not only does everything, including our brains and muscles, run on it, it's the glue that binds together everything in the multiverse. As we saw with the research of Brown, Wever and others, our bodies' own DC electrical fields interact with other fields, including the Earth's. Electromagnetism is crucial to understanding quantum physics, the "wave-particle duality" it specifies, and the "uncertainty principle": the fact that subatomic particles and waves are neither one nor the other until an observer like you or me looks at them. By extension, I think it's this principle that's behind us being able to psychically, albeit unconsciously, bring worlds together, as in our coffee-cup example.

It seemed perfectly logical that the boundaries of parallel worlds would be electromagnetic, and would produce measurable electromagnetic anomalies. And if it were possible to detect these boundaries, perhaps I could get a better grip on the nature of the paranormal in general and each case in particular.

The Case of the Almost Suicide

It was in the extraordinary case of the Uxbridge "suicide-to-be," centered in an 18th century farmhouse in that quaint Massachusetts town, that I first tested the idea that ghosts are essentially electrical. I had noted for years that home appliances seemed to be either targets or conduits of paranormal phenomena, particularly in poltergeist cases. The Uxbridge case, however, was to stimulate still more electrical questions.

I got the call from a friend of the afflicted family on a cold March day in 1983. I was in my office at *The Observer* in Smithfield, Rhode Island, where I was the managing editor. I turned up in Uxbridge the next day with my usual 35 mm camera, my tape recorder, and my brand new electromagnetic field (EMF) meter. An electrical-engineer friend had suggested this hand-held device, used to measure the alternating-current (AC) magnetic fields around electrical appliances and wiring. EMFs usually are measured in units called "gauss" (G) in the high range and/or "milligauss" (mG) in the low range.

"If you're looking for electromagnetic fields, this will tell you where they are," she'd said. "But I don't know about ghosts!"

EMF meters, which I note with a chuckle are often marketed to curiosity seekers today as "ghost detectors," are part of the standard kit for 21st century pop-paranormal research. I often talk with young ghost hunters, and few seem to fully understand EMFs and what relevance they might have as clues to the paranormal. In a society as drunk with technology as ours, the most common mistake is to think that gadgets can substitute for experience and instinct.

Depending on its sensitivity, any number of electrical sources can stimulate an EMF meter, even wires running along the insides of walls. Appliances, including microwave ovens and televisions; fuse boxes and fluorescent lights can too. Some of the highest readings will come from within six inches of appliances.

Typical would be a washing machine (100 mG), an electric mixer (600 mG), an electric stove (200 mG), and a blender (100 mG). Surprisingly, the heftiest readings I've ever had came from an electric can opener (1,500 mG), and an aquarium-filter pump (2,000 mG). The highest garden-variety reading within a house, but not near a man-made EMF source, would be about 6.5 mG.

My engineer friend had reminded me of my college physics: Some EMF fields are natural because the Earth is a huge electromagnetic generator. Geological and geotechnical factors can produce otherwise unexplained EMFs as strong as 500 mG. Further complications can come from radar installations, microwave towers or broadcast facilities even miles away.

So as I prepared to try my new tool in that rambling farmhouse, I realized that any useful EMF information would come by a process of elimination – a great deal of elimination, and still be risky. Nevertheless, I considered it safe to assume that, if the meter reading soared inexplicably in a limited area without proximity to obvious sources, there could be "somethin' strange in the neighborhood."

As soon as I saw the Uxbridge house on that drab March morning, I felt the depressing pull of its negative atmosphere. I parked in the muddy driveway. I hadn't even knocked when the back door flew open, and a heavy, forty-ish woman peered out at me. I'll call her Mary. As I entered the kitchen, a sniffly, wide-eyed four year-old, the only one of the woman's five children who wasn't in school that day, gaped at me from his seat at the table.

After I re-explained to Mary my first-visit, no-tell procedure (I had already done so on the telephone), I went back outside and circled the entire two-acre property. EMF meter on, there were several spots where I had readings of 300 mG or above, and there were a few places where I felt watched or even threatened by what seemed like non-human entities that were very aware of me. I snapped away with my camera. You could never tell when something my photo expert might call an anomaly would crop up – unexplained lights, objects that were invisible when the picture was taken, a face or, rarely, shadowy or even transparent figures. Occasionally, the camera would pick up what appeared to be one world superimposed over another, with no chance of the frame having been double-exposed.

Back inside, Mary led me nervously but quietly from room to room. The place was cluttered and in need of repair, but I felt no particular presences – yet. I snapped pictures at random, and I kept the EMF meter on. The needle hovered around 2 mG, a normal household reading. The living room seemed clear. So did the dining room. I toured the basement, and it was damp, dingy and debris-strewn, but not "hot" in the paranormal sense.

It was on the stairs to the second floor that things started to get weird. I was hit by a wave of that typical electrical tingling, and it was so strong that I almost became nauseous. Oddly, the EMF meter hardly twitched. Maybe what I commonly felt in these cases weren't EMF fields after all!

I snapped a few more pictures.

At the second-floor landing, adjacent to the upstairs bathroom, things got even more interesting. I could barely feel the tingle, but the EMF reading suddenly soared to nearly 600 mG. There wasn't an appliance in sight. What could the source be? EMFs have shape, depending on the current they wrap around, so I tried to trace this one's contour. I did so for a few feet, enough to see that the source wasn't in the wall or ceiling. It was in the hallway. And whatever this EMF source was, it was *moving*.

Oddly, I felt strongly that it wasn't an entity. Was it a world boundary…one that malign entities could cross? I strongly suspected that it was.

"Do you feel it yet?" my silent hostess, who had hesitated on

One of the odder photos from the Uxbridge, Massachusetts, farmhouse, taken while the author's EMF meter read "0," shows items not in the photo when taken with a 35mm SLR camera. For example, there was no light to the left, and there was only one lamp, the author says. There also was no "profile" as in the circle at right.

the landing, suddenly piped up.

At that moment, several things happened. Without warning, the meter dropped to zero. I at once felt something approach me from the other end of the hallway. I couldn't see it, but it was hostile, it was very strong, and it was very aware of me. After snapping a quick picture, I ducked into the bathroom – "out of the frying pan and into the fire"!

The presence – of the kind of creature I was already starting to think of as *parasitic* rather than demonic — stopped at the bathroom door, but it didn't enter. The bathroom itself was

The author believes these two photos are classic illustrations of overlapping worlds occupying the same space in the quantum "multiverse." In each, two or more rooms appear to overlap, but there are no overall characteristics of double exposure, "ghost images" or other known photographic anomalies. Both were taken in a Connecticut house where the residents are used to time slips and other odd occurrences that mesh with the author's theories.

alive with tingling, a horrible pall of depression, and a strong, female human presence. Somewhere in the multiverse, something terrible was happening to someone in this room! Much to my disappointment, the EMF needle barely budged. I would have an answer to that puzzle, but it would take a few more years and some digital technology.

I would get one hot clue two days later, however, after the pictures were developed. One photo taken in that hallway would have a plasma-like streak right where that anomalous EMF had been. I believe, and still do, that this is an actual photo of a world boundary. Other cases were to produce more such photos.

Meanwhile, confused by my EMF meter but concerned about this single mother and five children, I sat at the kitchen table and heard the story.

Mary, a registered nurse, rented the house, and she and her brood had lived there for over four years. They'd moved in just after the birth of the surprised little mite I'd seen at the kitchen table. She'd had a husband, but he'd long since left the family to "take off with a younger woman," Mary told me. Along with the four year-old, there were two girls, aged fifteen and thirteen, and two boys, ten and seven.

"There's always been something weird about this place, but the rent's cheap, and I needed the space for all the kids. The kids didn't really like the place, and none of them has ever wanted a room to themselves. They're scared to sleep alone."

By 1983 I was certain that the people in a troubled house always had as much to do with the phenomena as any paranormal entities did. I'd also learned that people never told me everything. I was still willing to come charging in with clergy and holy water if that's what people really wanted, but that wasn't only unreliable, it could well serve as a "quick fix" excuse for people not to get to the root of things, and solve the problems that were feeding the negativity in the first place.

Mary herself was preoccupied with work and family, and said she had seldom dated, or even had much of a social life, since her husband's flight a few years before. At one time or another, all members of the family had sensed presences, and had glance-over-your-shoulder feelings of being watched, sometimes by none-too-friendly eyes.

"But about two months ago, stuff started happening that was really scary. We started hearing and seeing things."

Mary described pounding on the ceilings and walls when nobody was in the adjoining rooms; foul smells from no obvious source; feeling the same malign presences I had, both indoors and out. Television sets, radios and stereo systems would switch on by themselves. The whole family heard footsteps from empty rooms, and sometimes they would see "shadow figures about the size of little kids."

Then "it" started coming after Eileen, the thirteen year-old.

"She'd wake up and start screaming at night. She said she could feel it touching her, and it would follow her to whatever room she was sleeping in and shake the bed."

Two nights before my first visit, it had torn the covers off Eileen's bed.

After the first two of my many lengthy visits, my conclusions were crystal clear. There were three, possibly four, of the entities I no longer thought of demons in the religious sense. I had come to think of them simply as parasites, non-human entities coming and going from their own parallel world(s) and feeding off people's negative energy. In this case, it was Eileen's negative energy. She eventually admitted that she and a friend had been "playing" with a Ouija board and that she at first rather liked the attention "the spirit" was giving her.

Other family members, completely disconnected from each other, also had lined up to be hot lunches for their uninvited alien guests. The older girl was full of pent-up resentment against her mother, blaming her for the father's departure. And the two older boys were focused entirely on themselves at the expense of family unity. The poor little four year-old felt unprotected and was clearly terrified.

As for Mary herself, she was a complete mess. While giving the impression of strength, she was a shambles inside – feeling absolutely alone, stressed beyond the breaking point, and cut off even from her children.

But two other facts told me there was still more "behind the scenes." First, it didn't seem that this family could pump out enough energy to feed three or four parasites. So a question popped into my head, one I'd never asked before but that I would never fail to ask again:

"Mary, what has your electric bill been like lately?"

She looked confused for a moment, then the light bulb (so to speak) came on.

"Funny you should bring that up. Since this crap started, the bill's been sky high most months, and for no reason I can see!"

In this and subsequent cases, I found that parasites often feed off the electrical system when they can't get people! But in the Uxbridge case, I had the nagging feeling that even that didn't fully answer the questions.

What about that poor, suffering human I'd felt in the upstairs bathroom?

I'd long since learned that the same factors at a site could feed unrelated phenomena. If the "ducks" were in order – EMFs, the right (or wrong) kinds of people – several seemingly unrelated worlds could converge, occupying the same space *without really coming together*. There could be parasites from one and the sights and sounds of ordinary people from others. These would be unrelated, but the situation often got extremely interesting and very complicated. That was especially true when the

The author believes that parasites can literally feed off household electrical systems. At this paranormally active Connecticut farmhouse, above, a plasma-like "orb" hovers around the exterior wiring. Below, orbs cluster around the exterior of a Rhode Island house where paranormal phenomena were actively occurring, and where the electric bill was excessive for no apparent reason. While many investigators believe that orbs are ghosts, the author is uncertain. He suspects several possibilities: That orbs are electromagnetic phenomena indicating the presence of parallel worlds and parasites, or actual plasma-based life forms.

parasites found their way into the "ghosts'" world as well as ours, or when the "ghosts" caught glimpses of us and thought we were ghosts haunting them!

I suspected that something like this might be happening in Uxbridge: That human presence felt like a suicide. When I asked Mary if she'd ever heard about a suicide in the house, her reaction was odd. She turned white as a sheet, gave me a "What are you really after?" look, then shook her head.

"There's never been a suicide here as far as I know," she replied.

A laborious search of local police and newspaper records showed that she was right. But what about a suicide in a close parallel world? What about a suicide in a world that to us would be the future? In the multiverse, it was very possible, and Mary's reaction to my question had been a clue.

She finally confessed that she herself had been contemplating suicide – in that bathroom and at such a time that an adult cousin – not the children – would have found her! Could that overwhelming presence have been Mary – in a simultaneous self — in that bathroom actually doing the deed? I think it's entirely possible, and I believe I've seen the same phenomenon in several cases since.

But there was even more. Early in my experiences of quantum reality, I became convinced that everything we are and everything we do sends out ripples through the multiverse, much like a rock thrown into a pond. The bigger the rock, the bigger the ripples. Traumatic, huge, emotionally ripping "rocks" like suicide, violent death, even great sorrow or burning hatred, send out vast shock waves across the worlds. So can positive "rocks" such as great triumph, love or happiness. That's at least one reason why some places are "happy" and others "sad" or even threatening. When we're there, we absorb some of the "ripples" coming off the positive or negative event.

At Uxbridge in 1983 I was absolutely certain that those parasites were attracted to and were feeding off the "ripples" from that act of suicide, whoever was committing it. The Uxbridge case convinced me that the principal method I had developed was correct, especially in parasite cases: Treat the cause, not the symptoms. The people and their negative energy and attitudes were the cause. The parasites and the bathroom "ghost" were the symptoms.

The treatment? Bring in positive energy to displace the negative energy.

I find it annoying that I have no handy scientific definition for either "positive energy" or "negative energy." In physics, of course, the terms can mean positively or negatively charged particles, theoretical concepts of mass, or simply whether or not something is above or below the zero point on a scale. But that doesn't explain how negative energy in the paranormal sense can bring or be brought by pessimism, hatred, illness, sorrow, anger, division or even stress – or how, under certain circumstances, it can attract and feed one or more of these alien creatures I call parasites. Nor does it explain how optimism, love, good attitudes, unity, honesty, mutual support and even humor can bring not only happiness and good health to people, but also can shut down the "food supply" to these nasty cosmic mosquitoes.

The more I worked with Mary and her family that year, the more I was convinced that it was indeed her in that bathroom, in the act of suicide in a close parallel world. That's because the more positive energy the family brought into their home, the weaker that suicidal presence became. It took nearly six months of visits and counseling to resolve this case.

Today I would never undertake such a task on my own; I'd have the help of the medical professionals who lend a hand when needed, or at least the aid of an appropriate, hand-picked member of the clergy, if I could find one. But Mary and her clan truly bonded with me, and they would talk with nobody else. That frequently happens to me with families having parasite trouble, and I've never decided if it's good or bad. Mary and her children did everything I suggested to bring in positive energy, and they worked very hard at it. They didn't become the perfect family – no family can – but they learned to stand together, lock arms, gain strength, and take charge of their own destiny. They even became more financially secure.

The suicide and the parasites faded into the background, the former to the point where it couldn't be noticed anymore. The critters, however, lived off the electrical system for a few weeks, then seem to have left for browner pastures.

As for my little EMF meter, I became convinced in subsequent cases that it really was picking up world boundaries, which seemed as fluid as the soap bubbles I'd already begun to use as analogies for the multiverse. By the 1990s, I had a digital EMF meter, and I finally found out why the needle on the old one often would drop to zero at and around world boundaries: Because the mG reading would fall into the negative range, which my old meter couldn't measure. This was very odd. It meant that, circumstances being right, the polarity of the EMF suddenly changed near these world boundaries, meaning that the energy flow had reversed. But where was it coming from and where was it going? If I was right, the energy was flowing between one parallel world and another!

West Virginia Outreach

An especially interesting example of this appears to have occurred in August 2003, when I was a speaker at the annual paranormal conference in Parkersburg, West Virginia. One warm evening I accompanied a large group by boat to the formidably named Blennerhassett Island Historical State Park, located in

The reconstructed mansion at the Blennerhassett Island Historical State Park, Parkersburg, West Virginia. While leading a "ghost walk" there, the author found what he believed to be electromagnetic connections between parallel worlds.

the Ohio River between the two states, for a "ghost walk."

From 1798 to 1811 this island was the site of the Harman Blennerhassett estate, on what was then the western frontier of the new United States of America. In a fine introduction by the park historian we were told that there were lots of history and several prominent ghosts. One of the latter was supposed to be Margaret Blennerhassett, lady of the manor who, before her own death, had taken to wandering along the riverbank in despair over the disappearance of her son.

I had always found ghost walks a little silly and, given what I was used to dealing with in my own work, somewhat boring. So imagine my surprise when the conference director (author, astrologer and psychic Susan Sheppard, who was to become a good friend) suddenly announced that, "Paul will be our fearless leader tonight!"

After an initial, "Huh? What?" I set off down the island's dirt road in the gathering dusk with some thirty ghost enthusiasts in tow. Susan and other local residents offered historical information as we went. As we arrived at a point near one of the estate's outbuildings, the group stopped to listen to some commentary. But I felt something strange, and it was behind us. I quietly made my way to the back of the group, and looked over a wide lawn that ran down to the river's edge, with the Ohio shore in the distance.

I couldn't see her, but there was someone on that lawn, someone in great emotional pain. I left the road and strode out onto the grass. Almost as an afterthought, I switched on my digital EMF meter. As I walked, then slowed and stopped, I got readings that fluctuated wildly from 230 mG to -300 mG, indicating to me a powerful, alternating-polarity EMF flowing, in my opinion, between where and when we were and where and when she was.

By this time the rest of the group had noticed what I was doing, and joined me. I almost never work in public, so it was an interesting experience being with this group, which included not only other ghost hunters and psychics, but some local healthcare professionals and two teachers with physics backgrounds. The surprised historian chimed in that this lawn was planted on fill. It had once been an inlet of the river, and this was one of the places where – you guessed it – Margaret Blennerhassett had walked in despair over her lost son.

I couldn't bring myself to leave this place without doing something for the poor woman. The group had already heard my theories about ghosts not being spirits of the dead but, among other things, actual people seen, heard and felt across world boundaries. They were willing to have a go at sending some positive energy her way. We held hands and concentrated, sending love and compassion back along that strange EMF. It seemed to me that the atmosphere lightened at once, and I knew we were perceived. Margaret, if that's who it was, almost certainly didn't realize that a crowd of caring people some 200 years in her future were throwing her a psychic/spiritual life jacket, but I'm certain that she felt an inexplicable lift.

Needless to say, my opinion of ghost walks rose accordingly! Throughout the 1980s and 1990s EMFs were a hot topic in the scientific press, not because they could be clues to the paranormal but because of health concerns. Technology had filled the world with artificially produced EMFs. It was already known that they could disrupt the brain's electrical activity during sleep. Could they cause cancer? Could they affect human cells or even alter DNA, as some scientists suspected? If so, at what levels and at what exposure?

Different studies often indicated different findings. Some researchers found a catalog of horrors, from cancer to heart disease to increased aggression to memory loss to disturbances in the Earth's electromagnetic Van Allen belts and weather anomalies, even birth defects, as a result of the riot of man-made EMFs we live in.

You know me…always the grand inquisitor! And as the 20th century came to an end, I had new kinds of questions.

Can locations where world boundaries converge for long periods, and houses within those locations, hold EMF health hazards for humans? What connection might these have to telltale cases of illness, especially chronic fatigue syndrome, that I'd seen among parasite victims? Can EMFs created by appliances actually *cause* parallel worlds to blend, or at least contribute to it? I certainly haven't the competence to answer these questions on my own. In 2005 I managed to corral my good friend Dr. Steve Cherry, M.D., to consult in the medical matters that come up, and that's a leap in the right direction.

The Paranormal Pooch

Affects of EMFs on animals have been documented as well. But they don't explain a fellow investigator I worked with during 2000: Wyatt, the world's only ghost-hunting dog!

Not knowing about his psychic talents, Jackie and I adopted Wyatt, a four year-old Australian Shepherd, simply because our boys wanted a dog. I'm a cat man from way back, but I gave in. Wyatt turned out to be personable, well-behaved and literally never barked. We never even knew what he sounded like until I accidentally stepped on his foot. He was civic-minded as well, doing a fine job of clearing the Canada geese off the local ball field each week.

But one day that spring I had a rather nasty case in Northbridge, Massachusetts, and I brought Wyatt along, intending to leave him in the car. There were several frightened children at the house in question, though, and they asked if Wyatt could come in and play with them. He was willing, but seemed very nervous as we entered the house, which I immediately felt was "hot" with paranormal energy, most of it negative.

Wyatt couldn't keep his mind on the children. Within a minute he had rushed down to the bathroom, where he stood shaking and alternately looking at me and the room. As soon as he saw that I'd noticed, he ran up the stairs to a bedroom on the second floor, doing the same thing and shaking all the while. We later found that there had been a suicide in that bathroom – within our own conscious past to boot – and that the person had lived in the bedroom Wyatt pinpointed.

The perky pooch saved me a pile of work!

Wyatt's ghost-hunting career was brief, however. I brought him in on a few other cases, but I quickly became worried about his nerves. To make matters worse, Jackie developed severe allergies, and Wyatt soon had to head for the unemploy-

Wyatt, the "ghost-hunting dog," with the author's sons in 2000.

ment line. It was a happy ending, though, as he moved in with the Rhode Island "rescue" lady for the Australian Shepherd breed's national organization, and he found a new life as a star in New England canine sports I had never heard of, such as "flyball" and agility courses.

As of this writing, we still have visitation rights.

Ghosts as Teachers

Questions about EMFs and other species having paranormal experiences, however, are utterly swallowed up by what I believe I've learned in this long spiritual and intellectual odyssey. God has become more real to me in ways I never expected. Ghosts, both human and non-human, not only make sense, they have become teachers. As individuals, as a species and as a civilization, challenges and dangers we haven't acknowledged in centuries face us out of the paranormal. The paranormal and its implications define what we are and what we can become. It is of immediate and vital concern to every man, woman and child on the planet. It is a map to the choices that will lead to humanity's ultimate destiny.

As I write this in 2005, our younger son, Benjamin, now thirteen, has joined in my paranormal adventures. Jackie and I considered very carefully before letting him get involved, but it has been a great success. Ben is very mature and very well balanced. He's great when there are young people involved with a case: He's very "in charge." Indeed, he has conquered something that terrifies most people, and that's a big plus for his self-esteem in this insecure and paranoid age.

What will Ben's personal odyssey be like? What breakthroughs and revelations will he see?

To find out where I believe we're all headed, we must take a new look at some things we're not used to looking at. We've looked at my journey; now it's time to look at God's.

God

3

In the

Image and Likeness

of Man

As a man is, so is his God....
-Johann Wolfgang von Goethe, *German Poet and Dramatist*

There's an eye-catching sculpture at the entrance to the Crystal Palace, an indoor amusement park in Dieppe, New Brunswick, Canada. It shows what we would look like if our body parts actually appeared the way our brains perceive them. The head, hands and feet are huge; the mouth, eyes and nose enormous. The whole thing looks like some self-centered troglodyte from a Gary Larson *Far Side*® cartoon.

Grownups raise their eyebrows when they see it. Children laugh. But if you think about it, the artist is right: It's very much the way we can appear to ourselves on the most visceral level. It shows how distorted our whole self-image can be without our even realizing it.

Now that we've entered the multiverse, it should be obvious that God, Whoever He, She, It or They may be, has cooked up a pretty strange, unexpected and gigantic Creation. One of the reasons we seldom appreciate it is that we're so self-centered: Most of us are just like that Canadian statue. I think it's from just such a distorted, selfish perception that most of us build our idea of God. Regardless of what our religions teach, we tend to see God not only in our own ways, but in terms of our individual needs, wants, prejudices, backgrounds and points of view.

Belief

Ask people anywhere outside the hardcore communist countries whether they believe in God, and you'll probably get a big "yes." According to a 2004 survey conducted for the British Broadcasting Corporation, belief in some form of Supreme Being is very high throughout the world, especially in Nigeria (100 percent) and the United States (91 percent).

There are exceptions, of course. An estimated 50 percent of Swedes are atheists (professed non-believers in God), and the Deity gets no public attention in officially atheistic societies like those in China, Vietnam and North Korea. But since atheists can't "prove" there is no God any more than believers can "prove" that there is, atheism is a matter of faith just as much as belief is, so I consider it a religion too.

There also are millions of agnostics throughout the world: People who aren't sure whether there's a God or not.

There's a perception that the more educated someone is, the less likely they are to believe in God. Nevertheless, a 2005 study by Rice University, Houston, found that some two-thirds of scientists are believers (as opposed to atheists or agnostics), although the raw statistics depend a great deal on what kind of scientists they are. Those in the social sciences – the ones who work most closely with people and human issues — are more likely to believe in God and belong to organized religious groups: some 69 percent. Only about 62 percent of those who work in the natural sciences claim to be believers.

Another 2005 study, this one from the University of Chicago, found that some 76 percent of medical doctors professed belief, with 59 percent acknowledging some sort of afterlife.

But what God do all these believers believe in? And how, if at all, can this belief – and God — relate to the quantum reality I'm convinced makes the worlds go 'round?

I've conducted my own "survey" on these questions for years, and the answers seem to have little to do with what organized religion, if any, the answerers associate themselves with. When it comes to God: The more educated the person, the more abstract the answers are likely to be…and the more likely the light bulb will go on when "quantum theology" (as we should start to call it) is proposed as a basis for understanding God's blueprint for the multiverse.

One of the more educated people around as I was writing this book was Sister Rita Larivee, SSA, a Roman Catholic theologian and publisher of the *National Catholic Reporter*. She started using the term quantum theology before I did.

"Everything is connected. Every thing has an effect on everything else. Nothing is in isolation. If I touch a flower that is springing from the earth, I am at the same time touching a star in the heavens above," Sister Rita wrote in 2004. "Quantum theology emphasizes the experience of the divine as told by the myriad of members making up the human experience, regardless of creed. It dismantles exclusivity so as to affirm that we are all connected."

The good nun hits the proverbial nail dead on, as we'll soon see!

From other believers with advanced academic degrees, I've

had everything from "God is the supreme but unknowable Creator and Guide of the universe" to "all-knowing, all-loving Father…or is it Mother?" One physicist told me cheerily that God is "coexistent with all time and conterminous with all space." Okay. Quantum physics makes that work!

Ye of Simple faith

Most workaday believers have no such grand visions. They generally adhere to religions, or at least religious traditions, because that's what their parents did. Many are the "salt of the Earth" and have great faith. Others seem to regard God as a sort of cosmic vending machine. If they go to the mosque on Friday, the temple on Saturday or the church on Sunday, things will go better for them in life, and they'll have a kind of insurance policy for the afterlife. Amid this group, I've encountered people who literally think that God is an old man with a white beard, rather like a celestial Santa Claus.

This group seldom questions its religious leaders. If its members change their affiliation, it's usually because of marriage to someone from another denomination or sect, and it's rarely outside the extended religion in which they grew up. Reformed Jews may become Orthodox Jews, and Baptists may "turn Catholic," but only rarely will a Hindu become a Muslim.

Even within extended religions, changes of affiliation can be too much of a reach. Within Muhammedanism, the two main branches, Sunnis and Shiites, consider each other heretical (meaning "wrong choice"), and rarely do the twain meet. And many scholars within both of these groups consider the three main lesser sects (Sufis, Harufis and Bektashis) heretical.

Ethnicism is very common in this group of believers. While blood is always thicker than water, many Muslim Arabs still look down on Christian Arabs as fake Arabs. Many Roman Catholics still call themselves "Irish Catholics" or "Polish Catholics" even though they belong to the same denomination. Despite the fact that a synod of the Eastern Orthodox Church condemned the heresy of phyletism (equating Orthodox Christianity and one's nationality) in 1872, some rank-and-file Greek Orthodox, Ukrainian Orthodox, Syrian Orthodox, Russian Orthodox, Bulgarian Orthodox, etc., etc., today are ferociously phyletistic.

I actually overheard this at a Russian Orthodox parish outing in Connecticut in 1976: "I love America. It's the only place I can be a Russian!"

I don't mean to sell short these simple believers, many of whom have the best of intentions and hearts of gold. And there is nothing wrong with a good, basic faith! My point about this group is that they're sometimes very out of sync with their own organized religions, even if those religions aren't all that organized.

Unbelief

What God do atheists *not* believe in? When I question them, a few will describe some goofy, stereotypical God that I don't believe in either. Many will try to broadside me with something like "no Supreme Being in any way, shape or form."

When I point out that there's a logical inconsistency there – that some force, personal or impersonal, "started the clock running" and governs the cycles of Nature, they will use terms like "blind chance" and fall back on dear old Charles Darwin (1809-1882), who came up with the original Theory of Evolution.

In return, I cite something like Sir Isaac Newton's laws of motion (indicating that there has to be a force behind all movement) and the fact that, statistically speaking, the Earth hasn't existed long enough for evolution to explain all the variations in Nature, let alone the existence of human beings. In the end, his or her faith put to the test, the atheist usually will laugh nervously, bluster in frustration, or perhaps admit that further reflection on the subject may be required.

Most atheists I know argue that religion has been responsible for most of humanity's blood-soaked history. They say that ridding ourselves of religion and other "superstitions" will make the world a much more peaceful place by eliminating differences in belief. This might be a tempting argument, but it ignores three things:

First, if people don't have religions, they'll find something else to fight over. Second, just because religions can cause political and social divisions – and not all do – doesn't mean there's no God. Because God – the real God – is all about what we're going to call "the Unity," divisions caused by religion only mean that religion sometimes has very little to do with God. And third, believing in, worshipping and loving God are as natural to people as eating and sleeping, and nothing is going to change that.

The vast majority of atheists I know seem to have axes to grind with the religions they grew up in, and, like most of us, with people who don't think the way they do. Whether or not they have academic degrees, most atheists strike me as two-dimensional thinkers and, to put it bluntly, narrow-minded and not too smart. I find them rather sad, cynical people, and I've never met one who honestly struck me as happy. I like to think that I have turned several avowed atheists into agnostics a least.

Atheists may claim not to believe in God, but I don't believe in atheists.

City Mouse, Country Mouse

Educated or not, there are fascinating differences in the way people perceive God from country to country. In poorer nations, where people see death frequently and generally have less control over their own lives, they tend to live in tightly-knit communities, be closer to the Earth, and belong to churches, mosques, temples or whatever. Some may have a close, even intimate, relationship with the divine. It's almost as if they need God more.

In developed nations, where people are more prosperous, rarely see death, and live in artificial environments that make them feel secure and in control, it's almost as if they think God needs *them*. People in these affluent, more urbanized settings tend to be more fragmented and less likely to belong to an organized religious group. They probably will believe in God, but sometimes as a faraway concept that has little to do with their own lives.

On the other hand, many believers in affluent nations feel the inner vacuum, and they develop deep spiritual lives without being associated with any standard religion, or with none at all. In these areas, mainstream Christian denominations are losing members in droves.

And this is where we encounter an interesting and, I believe, very important phenomenon that began in the late 20th century: the rise of "New Age" thinking and "neopaganism." The New Age movement is, on the surface at least, a highly individual search for self-fulfillment and spiritual growth outside traditional religion, and it tends to be strong in affluent nations, where lack of community, separation from the Earth, and social disaffection are most pronounced. New Agers have no central organization, but this diverse movement has inspired fresh interest in things spiritual, some novel philosophical speculation, and even a new genre in music.

Neopaganism is an outgrowth of the New Age movement and is an individual effort to return to one's own ancient pagan roots, or what people perceive as such. It's often driven by one's ethnic background. For example, neopagans of Scandinavian descent often try to rediscover that region's ancient worship of Odin. Neopagans of Chinese descent frequently try to revive traditional ways to honor their ancestors. Whether these revivals are entirely accurate is beside the point: "If it works for you, do it!" is the view. What matters is spiritual self-fulfillment.

We'll look more deeply at the New Age movement in our next chapter.

No matter where they're from, when people do adhere to an organized religion, they usually feel quite comfortable in it. At the same time, the average member of an organized religious group often will know little about the history, theology, beliefs, traditions (or at least the reasons behind them), and policies of their own religion. They might say they know, but their "knowledge" frequently is off by miles.

In fact, I think people remake their religions in their own images and feel perfectly comfortable doing so.

Mother is Never Forgotten

There is a particularly beautiful carved relief of the Goddess (of love and beauty) Hathor at her ancient temple in Dendera, Egypt. Muslim women who want children are sometimes seen at this image, leaving a vegetable offering and praying for the kindness of Hathor as "the mother of all children." This also occurs at several sites where there are images of the chief Egyptian Goddess, Isis, who was beloved throughout the ancient Mediterranean world. Isis is still worshipped today, here and there in one form or another.

Muhammedanism is a strictly monotheistic religion: Muslims believe in one God, and it's not Hathor. Are these Muslim women in Egypt simply ignorant about their own religion? Why would they risk official censure or worse to pray to an ancient pagan Goddess?

"I don't know who She is, but She is a good lady," is a typical answer. And they will tell you that the prayers work.

In another example, Christianity in its major modern forms

⇐
*Hathor at
Dendera, Egypt.*

⇒
*Isis, left, and
her consort,
Osiris*

officially condemns all attempts to communicate with the dead. Yet one can easily find Tarot card readers, psychics and mediums among practicing Christians, even in the strictest denominations. Asked how a person can, in good conscience, be a medium and a practicing Roman Catholic, or a Tarot reader and an evangelical "born-again," he or she will either sidestep the question or, in some cases, actually deny that their churches "really" forbid such practices.

There are plenty of educated people among rank-and-file believers, too, and they tend to worry about things. Educated Jews worry about anti-semitism and a perceived erosion of their population. Educated Muslims worry about God's name, their religion's image in the world, and backlashes against them because of terrorism. Educated Christians, with their religion's countless denominations, worry about everything: Bible infallibility, papal infallibility, liberals in the church, conservatives in the church, doctrinal minutiae, justification by faith vs. justification by works, dispensationalism, liturgical practice, the proper date of Easter, how to treat homosexuals, how to treat divorced people, what to do about clergy scandals, *The Da Vinci Code*, and so on *ad infinitum*.

And they all worry about each other.

Do All Religions Worship the Same God?

What about the religions themselves, as opposed to the people who belong to them? In the pluralistic societies of the developed world, especially in Europe and North America, a common belief among rank-and-file members of most religious groups is that "down deep, all religions are the same" or "all religions really worship the same God."

That may be true when it comes to a majority of ordinary believers. But when it comes to official religion, it's not true at all. Probably the most glaring rift between personal belief and official religious belief is, believe it or not, belief. While a large majority of people on the planet believe in a personal God, some of their religions don't. That's right – several major religions don't officially believe in God as the Creator or Ruler of the universe.

Buddhism, at an estimated 375 million adherents the world's sixth largest religion, doesn't acknowledge God either as Creator or Guide of the universe. It's almost entirely concerned with personal salvation through overcoming the failures of the world, especially human passions. Some ancient Buddhist philosophers, especially in the Mahayana tradition, actually condemned God-worship.

Hinduism, the fourth largest religion, with nearly a billion adherents, is actually a collection of polytheistic (worshipping more than one God) sects. Some will talk about "God" and some won't. There are myriad small religions and tribal faiths around the planet as well, most of them polytheistic.

Non-belief in God as Creator or Ruler goes all the way back to the 6th century B.C. in the old, but little, religion of Jainism, centered in India, with only about a million adherents.

But the Big Three — Christians, Jews and Muslims — worship the same God, right? Maybe and maybe not. Theologically it can be argued that they don't. While Muslims honor Jesus as a prophet, they certainly don't acknowledge him as literally God, as orthodox Christians do. Many Jews would balk at the idea that their God and the Muslims' Allah are one and the same. And there are Jewish and Muslim scholars who would say that the Christians' worship of the Holy Trinity — Jesus, as well as God the Father and God the Holy Spirit — makes them polytheists and pagans.

Even within Christianity there have, at times, been theological debates about whether the vengeful God of the Old Testament is the same as the loving God of the New Testament.

I could spend the rest of the book presenting these theological jousts.

So we have a certain fuzzy, but deep-seated, unity of belief across humanity, regardless of official religious doctrine. Like science, religion seems to create more questions than it answers. We seem no closer to solutions to: Who or what is God? What does it all mean?

Toward the Dawning of the Dawn

Something became very clear to me while studying theology: You can't get the right answers if you ask the wrong questions, or if you ask the right questions from the wrong point of view.

Perhaps the path to the answers we seek lies in changing our point of view. Perhaps if we turn away from the distorted, self-centered vision expressed in that funny Canadian sculpture, and that seems to typify humanity's overall picture of God, maybe we can get somewhere. Maybe we can ask the right questions.

I believe that if we "turn home" to our common point of origin – the beginning, the alpha point – of humanity and our mutual experience, things might get clearer. Maybe we can discover the One I will from now on call our Primal God. Oddly enough, I believe we must use the paranormal to help us make this discovery. And only then can we discover ourselves and our destiny.

"Hold on!" you might shout! "Who says there *was* a common point of origin? Didn't humanity start out in caves and end up in high-rises? Didn't we begin with Aristotle's *tabula rasa* and get smarter? How can we find answers to ultimate questions in a remote past that we not only know nothing about, but in which we were babies as a species?"

The idea that we started out primitive and stupid, and gradually got more sophisticated and smarter until we became the paragons of goodness and common sense we are today is a variation on the "linear" theory of history. Everything goes forward; things constantly get better, or at least more complex.

I think that theory is wrong, not to mention naïve. Growing evidence says that the "cyclical" theory is much more accurate. Things may start simple and get more complicated, but it all happens in fits and starts – and again and again. There are forward steps and backward steps. What goes around comes around. Things are uneven. At one period we can live in shacks but be intellectual giants. In another, we can conquer outer space but be spiritual bozos.

There's even archaeological and folklore evidence, controversial to be sure, that we have advanced from stone tools to power drills as many as four times in our long, virtually unknown prehistory, each time to be sent back to "square one" by a global natural disaster, a worldwide pandemic, or even war. After all, modern humans have been around for nearly 2 million years, and our known history goes back only about 8,000. That's an awful lot of empty time – time enough for a thousand civilizations to rise and fall.

In the words of British journalist and author Graham Hancock (1951-), who believes human history occurred much as described above, humans are "a species with amnesia."

I believe that too. It's not that we can't recall; we've simply accumulated so much baggage as a species that we don't consciously remember! I believe that our *subconscious* minds remember everything, mainly because *we're still there in one world or another in the multiverse*. But I think those memories also are embedded in our genes, our basic instincts and our deepest dreams, loves, hates and fears.

It's in the subconscious, and in what actually constitutes that subconscious, that our answer – and maybe our Primal God – actually abide. So I say again, there is a common point of origin, and we must look to our remotest past, a past that's an intimate part of us all, to find it. It's the Unity that forms the vast undercurrent in everything we are, do and believe. It's a Unity that, oddly enough, is our ultimate motivation as a species.

It brings us back to the popular claim that "down deep, we all worship the same God." And even that goes deeper.

4

The Quest for the One

We are born for cooperation, like the feet, the hands, the eyelids, and the upper and lower jaws.
-Marcus Aurelius, *Emperor of Rome, Philosopher*

Driving through the West Country of England on a mellow March evening in 1989, I happened upon a scene I'll never forget. The narrow country road curved around the bottom of a hill, where an old man and a young boy were driving a herd of cows through a break in a low hedgerow. Beyond the gate was a dirt lane leading toward a rambling house and some simple farm buildings. Behind it all the most glorious of sunsets was ablaze. It was like an old painting, awash with peace.

I pulled off the road and got out to take in the scene. The boy looked at me curiously. The old man smiled and put his hand to his cap in greeting.

"What a beautiful sunset!" I called across the sea of cows.

"Aye," he replied. "Not a bad sunset for such a little farm as this!"

I chuckled at such a cute quip, of course. But as the years passed it became a symbol to me of how people see the world. While that Canadian sculpture I described in the last chapter illustrates our distorted view of God, that little exchange on an English byway has been a symbol to me of our limited view of the world.

"It's a small world," we often hear, and most of us actually believe it. Some even take comfort in the thought.

But it's not a small world. It's the multiverse, and what a stupendous explosion of divine love must have created it!

Scientists look back into the deeps of space and time to the moment of what they call the "Big Bang," when all space, time, matter and energy as we know them were born. Evidently it was an ineffably bigger "bang" than our minds can possibly grasp. And it's to that event, generally believed to have occurred out of what physicists call a "gravitational singularity" about 14 billion years ago, that I believe we must look not only for the right answers but also for the right questions.

It began with that singularity (a point in space that has infinitely small mass but infinitely large density). It began with a literal and absolute Oneness. It began with the Unity. And I believe that the entire motivation behind everything Nature does, and everything that we and all our fellow creatures do, is a single-minded quest to get back to that primal Unity. I don't think we desire the impersonal unity of the singularity, but I do believe that the greatest underlying motivation – indeed thirst — of all life is to return home to a point of Unity in which we are Many but One, One but Many.

At first glance, and even at a second, that contention seems ridiculous. The whole point of Nature appears to be the proliferation of infinite variety and unending individuality, not to mention unceasing warfare for the survival of each. Over time, species change and diversify. Only rarely can members of different species mate and produce offspring, and even then their DNA must be very similar. The purpose of each creature seems to be the spread of its own genes at the expense of those of others. To this end, individuals, species, tribes, nations and empires battle to the death. The spilling of blood and the exaltation of the self, the individual, seem to be far stronger than any primal desire for Unity.

But if we look deeper, a different picture emerges.

Meet the Paradox

Life in the multiverse is full of paradoxes: things that seem contradictory but actually are true. The greatest paradox of all may be this: *The quest for Unity is the ultimate motivation for things that seem to destroy Unity.* Take any day anywhere in Nature and, if we really look, we can see this played out.

Plants struggle against each other for space, soil and sunlight. Insects, birds and animals compete for food, and sometimes devour each other. They vie for mates, and most struggle to protect their young. As Darwin contended, the strongest survive. But the paradox is here: By battling to survive, the individual – even the weakest one — serves the whole. Cruel as it may sound, when the weak are devoured, they become part of the strong. They die so the strong may prevail, and that strengthens an entire species because it helps the strongest genes survive. And because every species is an integral part of the biosphere (the entire interdependent community of life), the whole is strengthened.

Unity gets a little stronger.

Because our view of the world is so small, all we may see is the poor little squirrel being eaten by the cruel hawk. But we're actually witnessing an act of Unity: not a warm, fuzzy, gentle one by our standards, but still an act in service to the whole. That's why nothing in Nature is ever wasted. Everything nourishes something. Everything, no matter how humble, contributes to the strength and unity of the whole.

If we look even deeper, we might find that the multiverse itself is one big paradox: While it seems to be infinitely fragmented into diverse worlds, the multiverse may never have fragmented at all. That ultimate Unity may still be there, stronger than ever. That's because, as we see in even the simplest paranormal interactions, the multiverse's "bubble" worlds are not truly separate. They constantly interact as a unified system. Slips in time or space, big or little; seemingly random encounters with ghosts, UFOs, weird critters or whatever, aren't glitches or errors in the overall scheme of things. They're clues that the various worlds are not closed systems: The multiverse forms a grand Unity that only seems fragmented because we think – or have been snookered into believing – that it is.

Not only is our vision of the world too small. So is our vision of the multiverse. *And it's in realizing that this Unity is there after all that our journey to our destiny truly begins.*

Seeing and Not Seeing

Few segments of humanity are consciously aware of this Unity, and fewer still seem to realize that all humans were once aware of it, as I hope I will be able to show. Tribal shamans (priests and healers) know, as do the spiritually adept of many faiths and traditions. Legitimate mediums and psychics may not know the Unity as such or understand it, but many of them use it and live with it. When any of us has a paranormal experience, and we all have them regularly in one way or another, whether we know it or not, we are living it too.

In the deepest recesses of our spirits, maybe even in our DNA, I believe we all know the Unity. And we all thirst to realize the

Unity again, though not being able to put our finger on what it is we're actually looking for frustrates us to no end!

Some of us ordinary folks have begun to discover the Unity too, but we're not sure what to do about it, how to embrace it, what to do with it. We know that something is happening in the early 21st century, something the words "miraculous," "uplifting," "joyful" just can't capture.

I think our Primal God is returning from the shadows of the past.

The personal shock and breakthrough for each of us will come only with our discovery of the multiverse's greatest paradox of all, the key to understanding the Unity, and the door to knowledge about how and why everything works: *Our sense of self is an illusion whose true goal is to serve the whole.*

Once you achieve it, this one realization will transform everything about you, change the way you see everything, open your eyes in ways you never thought possible…indeed, open eyes you never thought you had. And it will give you power such as you never imagined existed.

I don't like to deal with "isms," but there are times when it's unavoidable. Before we continue our journey, we must realize the difference between "individualism" and "personalism."

The way it's used in this book, and with all due respect to the framers of the American Declaration of Independence, individualism is the self-centered quest for "life, liberty and the pursuit of happiness" *in isolation from others.* It's the spoiled, the-world-owes-me-a-living, screw-you attitude that's so apparent in post-industrial societies today. It's the inward-looking pursuit of self-gratification to the exclusion of all else.

It's a soul killer, and it makes itself and everyone around it miserable.

Personalism, on the other hand, is outward-looking. It sees the person as the fundamental component of reality, and it sees fellow people, and all creatures, as the other necessary components.

It's a world builder, and it touches everything around it with the power of potential.

The realization that the sense of self is an illusion does *not* destroy our own uniqueness. In another crucial paradox, this realization defines and fulfills our uniqueness. Realizing that we each are integral to the Unity fulfills our individuality.

Each of us is a unique expression of all of us.

We'll look at the hows, whys and full implications of this later. For now, the point is that when the human race doesn't realize, or even rejects, the Unity, we get what we see around us in the world now: division, hatred, destruction, chaos – death. Wherever and whenever there are factors that hinder or disavow the Unity, systems suffer and even collapse – whether they be planetary, social or personal.

The 'New Age'

Wherever you found this book, it may well have been listed or shelved in the "New Age" section. The New Age movement began in the late 20th century in response to the environmental crisis. With all its faults, it does promote respect for the Earth, personal spiritual and emotional growth, and human harmony.

One of the stimuli for this movement was the "Gaia Theory," advanced by James E. Lovelock (1919-), a distinguished British physician, philosopher and author considered by many as the spiritual father of the environmental movement. Whether he knew it or not, he was to become a major proponent for recapturing the Unity.

Named for an early Earth Goddess who personified the planet as mother of all life, the theory, originally known as the "Gaia Hypothesis," puts forth Earth as a unified system of interdependent life – the biosphere. While Lovelock stopped short of calling the planet and the biosphere a living superorganism, many believe the Gaia Theory amounts to this.

At the far edge of our knowledge there is evidence that, because the multiverse is a unified system, the biosphere embraces not just Earth but the entire multiverse. In this vision, matter, energy and consciousness flow freely among the worlds. What we call paranormal phenomena or "exceptional human experiences" not only are clues that the multiverse is there, but that it really is an open system, and that this universal flow indicates a deep, underlying Unity not only in all things *but in all possibilities*.

I'm convinced I've seen this flow on several levels, not only during the EMF experiments described in Chapter 2 but also in my own regular interaction with the paranormal.

Meet the Fractal

It might be a little easier to picture all this if we use "fractals." They're part of a relatively new view of mathematics known as Chaos Theory. Everything – even the multiverse itself – carries within it a copy of itself on every scale of size. Everywhere we look there are fractals! In outer space, galaxy clusters look like galaxies. A coastline seen from Earth orbit looks the same no matter how closely we view it. A broccoli "tree" looks like a miniature of the whole head of broccoli. And so on.

In the same way, the explosion of life all around us is a fractal of the explosion of that first singularity. Probably every world in the multiverse, no matter how different from any other, is nevertheless a fractal of every other. Perhaps each period in human existence has been a fractal of every other. Probably we ourselves are fractals of each other. And perhaps each of us is a fractal of our Primal God.

As we'll see in the "Ghosts" section just ahead, however, humans not only have suffered from factors that hinder or break the Unity, they often have embraced these factors and that break-age. That makes us primary among the biosphere's "flies in the ointment." While every other creature and thing naturally tends toward the Unity, we usually choose to embrace the non-exis-tent self, which promises a kind of fulfillment that doesn't exist either, and that just leaves us longing for more.

When we embrace individualism instead of personalism, we break the Unity of *the entire biosphere*. When we break the Unity, we mar our fractal nature, and we destabilize the multi-verse for every other creature and thing. We frustrate ourselves and everything else that exists. And we drive ourselves crazy either in trying to distract ourselves from this frustration through useless or destructive pursuits, or by wracking our brains about why we can't seem to achieve happiness.

Mitochondrial Eve

It didn't begin that way. There was, as we've said, a common beginning and a common purpose. Maybe that can help clarify our vision.

There's little genetic doubt that all humans alive today de-scend from one woman who lived in Africa about 150,000 years ago. We know about what scientists playfully dub "Mitochon-drial Eve" through the microscopic mitochondria in our bodies, which are passed only from mother to daughter, in this case over 1,500 centuries. That's about the time the DNA and fossil records indicate that the human race nearly died out from some disaster, probably an asteroid impact or the eruption of a "supervolcano," either of which would have filled the atmo-sphere with pulverized debris and blocked the sunlight for years, perhaps decades or even centuries. This would have obliterated most life on Earth.

Not only do we have a common ancestor, it appears that we really do have a common God.

Before the mid 20th century, anthropologists and scholars of religion assumed that humans started out as polytheists, worshippers of many gods and spirits. As nomadic bands of hunter-gatherers gave way to settled farming villages and large civilizations, it was believed that people became more sophisticated, with most finally working their way up to a belief in the one God. By mid-century, however, it began to appear that it happened the other way around. The picture changed thanks to the discovery of religious writings from the Sumerians, the earliest known civilization.

When the Sumerians' "cuneiform," at about 6,000 years old the earliest known form of writing, was first deciphered in 1835, it revealed a world of gods, goddesses, greater and lesser demons, and all sorts of spirits. All these beings seemed to engage in constant and terrible warfare, with humankind in the middle. But as earlier and earlier cuneiform tablets came to light, and the ability to translate them got better, an entirely different picture emerged. Instead of the unbridled polytheism of the later tablets, there appeared a rather elegant hierarchy of beings presided over by one God.

In 1931, near the end of his career, the eminent archaeologist and cuneiform scholar Stephen H. Langdon (1876-1937) of Oxford University was almost reluctant to publish these hard-to-believe findings.

"I may fail to carry conviction in concluding that both in Sumerian and Semitic (early Middle Eastern pagan) religions, monotheism preceded polytheism.... The evidence and reasons for this conclusion, so contrary to accepted and current views, have been set down with care and with the perception of adverse criticism."

Langdon eventually became convinced that the journey from monotheism to polytheism represented a steady deterioration in the human experience.

"In my opinion, the history of the oldest civilization of man (the Sumerians) is a rapid decline from monotheism to extreme polytheism and widespread belief in evil spirits. It is in a very true sense the history of the fall of man."

Remember this point. It's crucial.

The most ancient texts we have from the Semitic nations indicate the same trend at about the same times – between 5,000 and 8,000 years ago. These nations included the Assyrians, Babylonians, Canaanites, Chaldeans and other ancestors of the Jews and Arabs.

From the shadowy origins of Sumerian religion to about 3500 B.C., the number of gods in the Near East went from what appear to be three, headed by the Sky God Enlil, to some 5,000 entities of every ilk and attitude. Nevertheless, as more discoveries came to light, the more Langdon appeared to be right. The distinguished University of Chicago anthropologist Henri Frankfort (1897-1954) wrote during his Iraq excavations of the 1930s:

"We have obtained, to the best of our knowledge for the first time, religious material complete in its social setting.... For instance, we discover that the representations on cylinder seals, which are usually connected with various gods, can all be fitted into a consistent picture in which a single God worshiped in this temple forms the central figure. It seems, therefore, that at this early period His various aspects were not considered separate deities....

"This raises...the possibility that polytheism (arose)...because the attributes of a single God were differently emphasized by different people until those people in later years came to forget that they were speaking of the same Person. Thus, attributes of a single deity became a plurality of deities. It is not merely that single individuals laid emphasis upon different aspects of God's nature, but whole families and tribes seemed to have developed certain shared views about what was important in life and what was not, and therefore, not unnaturally, came to attribute to their god and to put special emphasis upon those characteristics which seemed to them of greatest significance."

Other scholars have traced evidence of monotheism to polytheism in ancient religions elsewhere, including Egypt, India, Asia, Africa, Australia, the Pacific islands and North America. Oral histories from Aborigine, Aka, Aztec, Berber, Carib, Dogon, Inuit, Khwe, Masai and Zulu all tell essentially the same Creation story.

Who Shattered God?

As always, this leaves us with many questions, the primary of which are: Who or What was this primeval Supreme Being? Was this God invented, discovered, implanted, or somehow always known? Was there a global religion in the remote past? And, most importantly, how – and why — did God get shattered into gods?

In this book we rely a great deal on circumstantial evidence: indirect clues that, when considered together, can form a clear picture. Among our most important circumstantial evidence is folklore or myth. Most of us today consider these as catch-all terms for stories, legends, fairy tales, and even jokes that have come down to us from the distant past. The big mistake we make is in assuming that folklore and myth are just quaint beliefs passed down from the ignorant ancestors of us geniuses, and that they never represent the truth.

Any student of folklore, however, will tell you that every tale or belief, no matter how outlandish to us or no matter how much baggage it has picked up over the millennia, began with some human experience, some shared event, some grain of truth. Rather than being enjoyable, but untrue, yarns we repeat around the campfire, folklore and myth carry ancient lessons and truths – even historical truths — through the ages.

Folklore and myth are the vessels of the collective memory of the human race.

Voices from the Dawn of Time

Fortunately the long-vanished Sumerians and their myths aren't our only clues about our Primal God. There exist today a few dwindling populations descended in unbroken line from the remote past, and in which prehistoric folklore remains a living thing. These include the San and Khoisan Bushmen of southern Africa, who still live a hunter-gatherer lifestyle, and whose genetics have been reliably traced directly back some 60,000 years at least. Their Y-chromosomes, the part of DNA that's passed from father to son, has been followed to about 150,000 years ago, right to the time of "Mitochondrial Eve" and the last mass-extinction event.

Not far behind the Bushmen are the isolated natives of the Andaman and Nicobar Islands in the Indian Ocean, whose genetics go back about 70,000 years. Then there are the Australian aborigines, with a continuous tribal life and oral tradition reaching back 30,000 years, and probably much further. Their very name means "from the origin." We can get a glimpse of our common beginning by looking at these three primal peoples, located in different parts of the world, whose religious beliefs predate those of the Sumerians by many millennia.

And when we look, we find a personal God, perhaps a bit misty, certainly with some animistic (surrounded by spirits) and anthropomorphic (given some human characteristics) baggage picked up over the ages, but a clear God nonetheless. Whether called Huve, Paluga, or Baiame, the Supreme Being walks serenely behind the prehistoric legends of these peoples. Usually thought of as having a wife and son, He presides over the "Dream Time" – the "Time before Time" — the era of Creation in which the Unity had not yet been forgotten. It was a time when all things were known to be conscious, and all living things could converse with each other. You could have talked with the trees and communed with the rocks.

What's more, it's a time still present in the many worlds of "dream" accessible by shamans, who can access these realms to help solve the hurts of our world and to learn from those who live in other worlds. And we see the multiverse and even the Gaia Theory in their original glory. It's a multiverse whose meaning is simply and beautifully expressed in primal human belief systems such as the Africans' *Ubuntu*: Everything I do affects you. Everything you do affects me. And everything we do affects the whole world. Indeed, it affects all the worlds.

What these "primitive" peoples and their prehistoric legends describe is the multiverse as an open and unified system, and as our Primal God's blueprint for, and map of, reality. It describes the Unity as the guide on how to live life, and the path to truth and fulfillment.

Life for these elder peoples takes unimaginably varied forms – us, insects, animals, trees, ancestors, spirits, gods, goddesses, godlings, demons, ghosts, spirit guardians, monsters, and it flows freely among a myriad of worlds. It's all a vast, interdependent reality full of friends, enemies and answers. It's a multiverse where the paranormal is entirely normal. It's an infinite diversity that forms the perfect Unity. It's one world made up of many worlds that can be used if one only knows how.

This appears to have been our common world at the beginning.

In this primal world where Unity still rules, God is the Unifier, the Starting Point and the Goal. God is the One Who shows the way and makes things as they should be. God is not the result of the Unity, God is the Unity. God is Reality. God is, so to speak, the First Fractal. But God also is the two primary forces of life – the male and female principles, in balance and fertile with new life. In these primal religions, God is Father (represented by the sky), and Mother (represented by the Earth). Their love produced a Child (us or a god representing us).

But to these children of the human dawn, God is not just a symbol for the powers of Nature. God is the soul of Nature, God is a Person intimately close to us — closer to us than we are to ourselves.

Since the family is the basic unit of human society, indeed human existence and survival, these original people seem to have seen our families as simple and beautiful fractals of God. While we moderns have remade God in our own image because we are broken from the Unity and no longer have a clue, maybe our remotest ancestors realized that we really are made in God's image. And behind all their beliefs is a prophecy that somehow, somewhen, the Dream Time, the Unity would be realized once again.

While we may be, as Hancock points out, a "species with amnesia," our Primal God hasn't been entirely lost, and can't be as long as we're human. The name we so arrogantly give our species, *Homo Sapiens* (Knowing Man) is a misnomer because we hardly "know" anything, let alone ourselves. Much more accurately, we are *Homo Adorans* (Worshipping Man). God is in our genes. The often-abused term "God's will," means one thing: That we each return to God, the Heart of the Unity. Down deep, even our modern religions remember the existence of many worlds, and that one ultimate goal of existence: the return to the Unity.

From the *Bhagavad-Gita* ("Song of God") of the Hindus:

"I instructed the imperishable science of uniting the individual consciousness with the Ultimate Consciousness...." (Chapter 4:1)

"...With your consciousness absorbed in Me, taking complete shelter in Me, executing the science of uniting the individual consciousness with the Ultimate Consciousness, you will be able to know Me completely, free from doubt." (Chapter 7:1)

"...there are many worlds of the living and the dead. Pierce them all through love at the last moment when the great transition (death) comes, be only in Me. (*The Bhagavad Gita and Inner Transformation*)

And the disturbing, "I am become Death, the destroyer of worlds...." (11:32).

From the Jewish Torah and Christian Old Testament (claimed by Daniel M. Berry of the University of Waterloo to be the correct translation):

"In *a* beginning, God created the heavens and the Earth...."

From the Christian New Testament:

"But in this the final age He has spoken to us in his Son...and through Him He created the worlds." (*Hebrews* 1:2)

"I am the Alpha and Omega, the Beginning and the Ending, says the Lord, Who is and Who was and Who is to come, the Almighty." (*Revelation* 1:7-8)

Father and Mother

Sometimes the primal faith is remembered in the most unlikely places, including two of the most ferociously male-oriented religions in history: Judaism and Christianity. Just as in the primordial Bushmen religion, with Huve having a wife and son, Yahweh had a female counterpart in ancient Judaism. She was known as the Shekinah. Even the Prophet Isaiah refers to the Shekinah with feminine pronouns (*Isaiah* 51:9-10). And us? We are all "sons of God," according to the Torah.

In Christianity, the notion of the Holy Trinity (Father, Son and Holy Spirit) is not unique. It is a reflection of the primal divine family as experienced in many other and far older religions. Theologically, the Holy Spirit has feminine characteristics, and is personified in the Bible as "Chokma" and "Sophia," Hebrew and Greek, respectively, for Wisdom. Both are feminine words. This is all through the Bible, especially in *Proverbs* (8 and 9) and even in the New Testament (*Matthew* 11:19, *Luke* 7:35, and much more). And us? Jesus, who theologically is fully God and fully man, is the "Son of Man" in the New Testament. He, too, is us.

In modern times, the break from our Primal God, and thus from the Unity, has had deadly consequences for our vision, our society, our lives and our planet. And some scientists, philosophers and theologians have known it.

Pierre Teilhard de Chardin (1881-1955), who was all of the above and a controversial Roman Catholic priest to boot, may have been a little shaky on the many-worlds thing, but he saw the break with the Unity as a break with God and with what humans are meant to be.

A French Jesuit, Teilhard was a paleontologist, biologist, philosopher, mystic, and one of the greatest visionaries of the 20th century. His lifelong motivation was to reconcile natural science (especially the Theory of Evolution) with religion, specifically Christianity. His studies led him directly to the idea of humans as creatures of endless possibility whose ultimate destination was the "Omega Point": a total reuniting of all things in the consciousness of God.

Decades before the environmental movement or the Gaia Theory, Teilhard saw this ultimate Unity as the whole point of life and the Earth, which he characterized as having its own personality and spirit.

"The Age of Nations is past. The task before us now, if we would not perish, is to build the Earth," he wrote.

He clearly saw our modern separation from the Earth as a symptom of separation from God and the disunity of all things.

"We have reached a crossroads in human evolution where the only road which leads forward is towards a common passion....

To continue to place our hopes in a social order achieved by external violence would simply amount to our giving up all hope of carrying the Spirit of the Earth to its limits."

All very nice words, maybe, especially if you're not poor, hungry, sick or abused. But what does it all really mean for us? I don't think we're ready to handle that just yet.

For now, suffice it to grasp that, for us and our relationship with God, Teilhard's "Spirit of the Earth" was broken at some point early in our history. What happened? What disease did we catch? Whatever it was broke the Unity for us, affected the whole of Nature and, ultimately, the entire multiverse.

I ask again: Why and how did our Primal God become 5,000 gods, goddesses, demons and spirits? And again, I believe we must turn for an answer to folklore and myth, for these indicate clearly that the relationship of humans to the whole was disrupted by what can only be called "outside influences." And this is where we again meet the paranormal head on, and in a way that I believe has life-or-death lessons for the modern world.

Until we probe what happened to our ancestors, we will never understand why we are the way we are, or why we perceive God the way we do. We will never grasp why our relationship with God is broken or how to touch our fingertips to God's once again. We will never find out how to realize the Unity and save ourselves.

For more answers, we must leave our Primal God for awhile and plunge into the paranormal in a way few people save the ancients and the shamans have ever done.

Ghosts

5

Enemies: Divide and Conquer

Turning and turning in the widening gyre
The falcon cannot hear the falconer;
Things fall apart; the centre cannot hold;
Mere anarchy is loosed upon the world,
The blood-dimmed tide is loosed, and everywhere
The ceremony of innocence is drowned;
The best lack all conviction, while the worst
Are full of passionate intensity.
Surely some revelation is at hand....
- William Butler Yeats, *Irish Poet,*
From *The Second Coming*

We now enter the strangest and most disconcerting part of the story of our species, and of our relationships with each other and with God. What I present here isn't even known, let alone taken seriously, by mainstream scientists, though it may be silently suspected by some. Few theologians and philosophers are willing to deal with it. It is, once again, based on circumstantial evidence. And, as God is my witness, I hope the overall conclusion is wrong. But if not it will explain much about our history and, if we can get some control of it, do much to determine our destiny.

Those who accept anything close to what's suggested in this chapter often are honest-to-goodness religious fanatics. Others are pseudoscience buffs with little or no training in how to interpret archaeological or anthropological clues in context. Skeptics might cheerfully stick me in the second category, and they might be right. But neither they nor those they'd stick me with have been in the paranormal "trenches" with me for the past thirty-six years, seeing it first hand.

The thing has two parts, and I don't know which one is worse.

The Parasite Factor

In the last chapter I suggested that there had been "outside influences" on our religions and our prehistory, that our story was taking us right back into the arms of the paranormal, and that we once again had to use folklore and myth for an answer about what happened to our Primal God and to ourselves.

Henri Frankfort's contention was that God's attributes became "differently emphasized by different people until those people...came to forget that they were speaking of the same Person. Thus, attributes of a single deity became a plurality of deities." While this is a sensible analysis, Frankfort didn't go far enough. Why should he? Frankfort never saw first-hand what parasites out of the multiverse can do to people.

Parasites. Remember them from Chapter 2, when I encountered them in the most negative, indeed "demonic," of my cases? I believe that parasites are the first part of our answer about what went wrong. It took decades of studying and, often enough, battling these hungry, hostile, half-tangible creatures from elsewhere to form the conclusions I espouse here.

So let's start with our familiar tools, myth and folklore.

The Primal God isn't the only being who filters down from distant ages in the tales and dreams of the most ancient peoples. There are a multitude of other beings, some human and some very far from it. Most were and are considered spirits (beings without physical bodies), though I think this is wholly inadequate. Most of the entities "viewed" or "felt" across what I have called the multiverse's "world boundaries" usually have physical characteristics and certainly can have physical affects, intended or not, on our conscious world.

Why shouldn't there be worlds upon worlds of other beings? Even if they don't accept our interpretation of the multiverse, scientists keep finding hints of what "primitive" religion already knew: Our vision of life is ludicrously small. In fact, life is incredibly tenacious, stunningly diverse, and it's simply everywhere. Living microbes have been found in the cores of nuclear reactors. Can you imagine a more hostile environment? Frozen microbes found in a buried Antarctic lake, and believed to be nearly 3,000 years old, were revived in 2002 simply by thawing and adding water! And there are many unconfirmed reports (unconfirmed because trained scientists weren't present) of dormant insects, amphibians and other creatures found in hollow rocks millions of years old, and revived.

In the late 1970s undersea researchers off South America excitedly announced the discovery of volcanic (geothermal) vents on the ocean floor. In ensuing years scientists have found more and more of these sites, at which seawater that has seeped down to the molten rock far below is superheated and forced back through the vents into the sea. Biologists, who had always assumed that the sun was what ultimately powered all biology on Earth, were flummoxed to discover hundreds of new species around these vents. They were entirely unknown life forms dependent not on the sun, as we are, but on (to us) deadly hydrogen sulfide.

The great British astrophysicist and author Sir Fred Hoyle (1915-2001), honored for his work by everyone from his scientific colleagues to Queen Elizabeth II, was convinced that life is not the fragile exception in the universe, as most of us have been taught to believe, but the unquenchable rule. He even believed that the vast "gas clouds" seen by astronomers in space actually are clouds of microbes that "seed" planets with life, a theory known as panspermia.

Today, NASA actively searches Mars for "life as we know it." But what about life as we *don't* know it? What about the multiverse, that infinte sea of worlds that touch, pass through one another and even combine, right at the edges of our consciousness? They give us "exceptional human experiences" and, in turn, our myth and folklore – stories of life forms not native to our own tiny corner of the multiverse; endless varieties of life that our immediate ancestors called ghosts, demons, fairies, spirits and, yes, gods and goddesses. Our ancestors knew the multiverse as the true world, and their shamans knew how to use it to help their people.

Sir Fred didn't know the half of it.

From one or more of these worlds come what I call parasites, the source of some our most primal myths, and they are where our explanation for how God became gods – and why we are the way we are today – must begin.

That parasites are responsible for our primordial legends of evil spirits, demons, etc. should be obvious. But it doesn't end there. Notice that from the ancient Near East, Asia and the Americas come the oldest tales of vampires: stories not of blood-sucking guys in capes, but of "life-sucking ghosts." While that term is known today mostly in video games, paranormal investigators meet the real thing all the time, whether they realize it or not.

In human myth-memory, parasites were the prototypes for vampires.

In previous books I describe many of my own encounters with these parasites. As a matter of fact I've encountered them so often that I can, as the cliché goes, "smell them a mile away." Here's what I know.

Parasites aren't native to our part of the multiverse. They're not the spirits of dead people, nor are they the psychic "remnants" or "residue" of anything. They're not "fallen angels" or "servants of Satan." They're life forms just as we are, but they're different in many ways, and there even seem to be several different species.

Parasites are highly intelligent, and they're quick learners. I've known "rogue" parasites, and I've known others that hunt in packs. I've encountered several that have attached themselves to families for generations. They often pretend to be deceased loved ones, "spirit guides" and even angels. Some species appear to have gender. Parasites have a certain conscious mobility among worlds that most of us do not. As a result, in their more extreme manifestations to us, they appear to be able to manipulate space and time to a certain degree.

If you want to call parasites "aliens," you won't be wrong.

I suspect a great deal more.

Humans are carbon-based life forms. But parasites, which may be just as physical as we are in their own worlds, seem to be based on plasma (ionized gas or electrified air molecules). Most parasites even look like plasma in one form or another, both in photographs and on the rare occasions I see them with the naked eye. Some species appear smoky, either light or dark. Others look very bright, almost like bolts of lightning. Still other kinds appear as shadowy figures, some nearly solid. Some can be quite disconcertingly solid, though this is rare.

They may appear in these forms not because it's what they

During a 2005 case in Vermont, Benjamin Eno captured this shot of what the author believes is a parasite standing behind this man's right shoulder. The entity's "shoulder" is so dense that it blocks out part of the framed document and shelving in the background.

actually look like but because, in many cases, their energy is simply reaching into our reality. They or their "feelers" may simply be "riding," for lack of a better term, the inter-world electrical currents that hold the multiverse together, as we saw in Chapter 2. The more solid they appear, the more they may actually be "in" our reality.

I've seen indications that many parasites not only are organized but have a social structure, with clear leaders, and perhaps even a culture. Most seem extremely long-lived, but I believe parasites can and do "die" in whatever sense death can be possible in a multiverse where every creature is not only present in myriad worlds but also shares the life of every other creature. Any notion of death for creatures that can consciously move, or at least act, between worlds is slippery at best.

The existence of plasma-based life forms already has been theorized by astrobiologists (scientists who speculate about alien life). That's the kind of fluidity that would help parasites ride, or at least use, electrical currents that happen to cross world boundaries. Because of its ionized state, plasma is extremely conductive, and it can interact dramatically with the electromagnetic fields (EMFs) we discussed in Chapter 2 as being associated with them.

Why do parasites hop among worlds, and why would they pretend to be your late Aunt Gertrude? For the same reason you pack the kids into the car and ride to the fast-food joint: to eat. Parasites' livelihood seems to be gained entirely by riding or reaching from world to world to feed upon the likes of us, and probably other creatures we know nothing about.

What is it they're "eating"? Apparently, some sort of negative energy produced by humans. All I know is that they thrive on whatever energy we put out when we're divided, stressed, angry and full of hate. When we're united, calm, happy and full of love, parasites not only lose their "food supply," most seem positively repelled.

One answer may lie in cognitive neuroscience and the study of those little, oscillating electrical voltages all our brains produce. Of the four types of brain waves (alpha, beta, delta and theta) measurable on an electroencephalograph (EEG), beta waves are most present during situations of stress and anger. Do beta waves "ring the dinner bell" for parasites? Possibly. And if victims don't provide enough sustenance on their own, parasites have ways to prod them into doing so, almost like us squeezing an orange to get every drop. Hence, you get stressed, frightened and angry when something starts tossing around your fine china, or when you become convinced that Aunt Gertrude is hanging around to punish you for wasting the money she left you, or for giving away her goldfish. The more frazzled you and your family get, the more "food" you produce for your unwanted guests.

As with humans, parasites are amazingly "psychic," but their belief systems haven't denied and buried this crucial survival tool. And why shouldn't parasites be psychic? From our viewpoint, "psychic" means perceiving more than one world at a time, and they obviously can do that.

Parasites quickly learn which "buttons" to push to excite not only more fear and anger in individual victims, but in whole families. Division – attacking all trends toward the Unity, if you prefer – is their greatest hunting tool. If they get strong enough, they can engage in communication, including audible verbal abuse of people, and even physical attacks. This, of course, can turn the parasite into the nasty and far more familiar poltergeist (from two German words meaning "noisy spirit").

Taken to its frozen limit, I've seen victims actually bond with parasites to the point that what has been known in folklore as "demonic possession" can result. It reminds me of hostages who actually bond with their captors, a phenomenon sometimes seen in terrorist situations, and even join them on rare occasions!

Oddly enough, if the typical parasite victim drastically changes daily habits or sleeps in a different room, the parasite sometimes has trouble locating him or her for days or even weeks. While parasites can slip between worlds, their mobility while in ours often seems strictly limited.

As suggested in Chapter 2, many factors must line up for any human-parasite connection to occur. Along with a "food" source, there have to be inter-world electrical currents and EMFs that parasites can ride to get here. And these currents, in turn, depend on many factors, including site geology: The more electricity the site can conduct because of high water tables, sandy or clay soils, etc., the easier it is for the paranormal to manifest.

Speaking of EMFs, what role today's global electropollution plays in enabling parasite activities is an open, and pretty scary, question. Unless we live in the Australian desert, all of us are awash in man-made microwaves and EMFs of many strengths virtually all day, every day. What this is doing to us physically and emotionally is unknown, but what it might be doing to parasite capabilities isn't even being discussed.

In folklore, ghosts often are associated with places where murders, suicides and other highly charged events have occurred. This is another example of myth as a vessel of race memory. If the factors are right, parasites are definitely attracted, *not necessarily to the place but to the event*, even if it's happening at the site in a part of the multiverse that to us is the future. Remember our would-be suicide in Chapter 2?

What's more, many parasites feeding on such an event seem able to operate freely in other worlds at the same site.

The Prussian Parasite

A textbook case occurred in 2004 in King of Prussia, Pennsylvania, not far from Philadelphia. This critter showcased not only the intelligence and quantum versatility of the typical parasite but, crucially, the case demonstrated our own ability to fight back.

The call came October 6th in an e-mail, and it so happened that I was going to be in Philadelphia for a conference later that month. Once at the site, I checked the house with my usual preliminary methods, concluding that a parasite was indeed at work. Afterward, here's the story I heard.

"Weird things have been happening to Kate, and the night before I e-mailed you I saw first hand how weird it is. I've never seen her so afraid," stated the young boyfriend I'll call Chuck.

"It's like somebody sits on my chest and I can't breathe," Kate added. "I can't move or speak."

Kate and her sister, Carmen, had moved into the small, rented house about a year before, and the trouble had started about four months later as is typical: soft footsteps on the floor above. As the girls had become more frightened and frustrated, the parasite had gained strength, pounding on walls and starting the night attacks. Kate seemed to be the prime target.

"Everything stopped for a few weeks after Kate moved her room upstairs, and she seemed like her old self again. But now it's after her again and she has no energy. She's exhausted all the time," Chuck explained.

There had also been minor poltergeist activity, including a floating ashtray. And there were voices.

"Three nights ago, Carmen and Kate were in the living room, and Carmen saw something whitish and smoky hanging over Kate. Carmen said, 'What the hell?' Then the damn thing floated over to Carmen and she heard a man's rough voice, 'Don't you f***ing move, you bitch!' and something started pounding on the walls!"

Both girls screamed, and they fled the house then and there. They'd stayed with friends until I arrived that day. In my preliminary examination, I had sensed only one parasite, but quite a strong one. And there was something else, something in the tiny yard at the back of the house. On that little, empty lawn, an event was happening elsewhere and elsewhen in the multiverse. I could almost hear a woman screaming, and I could practically see the deliberate gunshot that had killed her husband. And the parasite could feel it too, indeed was feeding off it. But as it did so, it also reached into other accessible worlds, like some sort of electromagnetic octopus from a horror movie.

And it had found Kate.

Eventually this case was resolved by the girls learning to understand, rather than fear, what was happening, building up positive energy and compassion, then directing it all toward that event in the yard. Within a few weeks, it worked.

"We knew there was something weird about the yard," Sara told me. "But when we started sending love at it, that bad energy would turn off like a light switch!"

There was much more to this case, of course, but my point is that, in order to sustain themselves, parasites can communicate, manipulate and exacerbate in all sorts of ingenious ways. One especially effective, and very common, parasite trick in a household is to mimic the voice of one family member and say obscene or insulting things to another family member, and *vice versa*. From a parasite's point of view, you can imagine the quick results this can have! Sounds like something right out of a "sitcom," but I assure you there's nothing funny about it.

The God Connection

So what does all this have to do with God?

Everything.

What one or more parasites can do in a family, why couldn't

they do with a tribe or village, especially when those tribesmen or villagers already had some realization of the multiverse and its interdependent life?

Can you imagine the sustenance – the power — a parasite, or even an organized troop of them, could gain by manipulating and communicating with a group of humans until the people thought they were hearing from a super being: a god or gods? Imagine the negative energy – the "food" — generated by human fear on a tribal or national scale. Think of the impact across the worlds of the barbarism we fell into as our God split into god after god after god, many of which, according to both folklore and archaeology, demanded human blood. Consider the negative power of torture, of human sacrifice. Consider the power of war.

I'm the last one to claim absolution or even "temporary insanity," either for individuals or our whole species, because we may have been duped by parasites. And I would never advocate the surrender of responsibility, personal or communal, because of any influence by these wretched cosmic beasts. As we were suckered out of the primal, multiversal unity of the "Dream Time," and we lurched headlong into a world of division and death, we knew exactly what we were doing. The "buttons" of ignorance, greed, lust and individualism were used against us.

With their own keen intelligence, parasites used and still use our worst tendencies to break the Unity, drive us apart, and line us up as hot lunches so they can get even stronger. We as a species were and are quite literally being farmed.

As Frankfort stated more aptly than he realized, the history of our estrangement from the Unity; of the splintering of our lives, world views and societies; of the division of our Primal God into many gods, "is in a very true sense the history of the fall of man." What could be more evil than that? Folklore or not, parasites have truly earned their reputation as "demons."

I'm often asked if parasites could be humans – or former humans — who feed upon others from whatever worlds their conscious minds have ended up in. After all, each of us knows plenty of vampiristic people! While such a scenario seems perfectly logical, I must say that I've never encountered a parasite that "felt" to me to be the slightest bit human. I find that reassuring. On the other hand, I could be misinterpreting my own impressions – an accusation I frequently hurl at psychics and mediums. Perhaps at least some of these creatures were human, but there's so little humanity left as to leave them unidentifiable.

There are plenty of modern examples of what might be significant parasite influence, both inside and outside religion.

The sophisticated modern Jew, Christian or Muslim might say, "Ahh Haaa!" and point a finger toward Voodoo, Santeria or other animistic religions in which people often deal with "spirits" and are sometimes very much under their influence.

I have my suspicions in that direction, too, but I also think that people who point fingers ought to look in the mirror first. The 1994 Hebron mosque massacre by a Jewish radical (and other Israeli atrocities against Palestinians), the Roman Catholic Church's "Spanish Inquisition" (which didn't end until 1834), the Holocaust against the Jews by the Nazis (who expected people to believe they were defending "Christian civilization"), and the ceaseless bloodletting carried out by Muslim terrorists in the name of Allah (no elaboration necessary) were not inspired by any God I worship.

All of us have blood on our hands, and I see our Primal God nowhere in it. I have no doubt that parasites see human religion as, in a manner of speaking, one of the most convenient utensils in their kitchen drawers.

The Bell Witch

There are examples of parasites' sway that go way beyond religion. Probably the most graphic illustration of a parasite's influence over an entire community in modern times is the famous "Bell Witch" of Tennessee, basis for the 2006 film *An American Haunting*, with Donald Sutherland and Sissy Spacek. This incredibly bizarre series of events, which centered on the Bell Family of Adams, Tennessee, from 1817 to 1821, is the most famous poltergeist story in American history. It has variations, but there is enough documentation, including eyewitness testimony, in the written history of Robertson County to convince me that most of the story happened as told.

What most listeners encounter in the Bell Witch story is one nasty poltergeist that centered on young Betsy Bell, then harassed her elderly father until he died. The Bell Witch is touted as the only documented case in which a "spirit" actually killed anyone, a claim I take serious issue with.

What I encounter is the story of as many as four famished, brilliant and vicious parasites that found "all the ducks in line" for a feast in a family in which, one document indicates, child sexual abuse was taking place. These always-invisible entities, which acted as one most but not all the time, developed such power and personality that they dominated not only the Bell Family, but actually gained friends and power throughout the area.

They did this quite literally through politics. As the story of the "witch's" antics in the Bell home spread, people came from far and wide to see it and hear it. The visitors supposedly included Tennessean and future U.S. President Andrew Jackson and his entourage. Reportedly the parasites would tell hilarious jokes, predict the future, quote from the Bible, and together had a very sweet singing voice. Self-righteous churchgoers should take note of the fact that the "Bell Witch," known locally as

"Old Kate," apparently never missed Sunday divine services —
in several different churches at once! "She" could repeat the
sermons from each church word-for-word.

The entities, which professed affection for many members of
the community, humorous derision for others, and strong dis-
like for a few, drew more and more attention as they got stronger and stronger. By this time the entities were moving freely
about the county, gave helpful agricultural and financial advice,
and even engaged in matchmaking! At one point "Old Kate"
reportedly saved the life of a little boy caught in a cave-in.
Despite these positive acts it was hard to catch the "Bell Witch"
telling the truth. "She" would send people off on wild-goose-
chase treasure hunts, for example, then laugh at, and no doubt
feed upon, the results. And the entities knew everybody's private business, often setting people against one another.

With this combination of unceasing attention going to the parasites, and a keep-'em-guessing mixture of magnanimity, humor
and nastiness coming from them, this scenario has "tribal god"
written all over it. Had this not been a strict, 19th century Prot-
estant community, the "Bell Witch" might easily, and quite literally, have taken over.

As a matter of fact the "Bell Witch" might well have been a
set of unemployed tribal gods.

Long before the Bells or any other European-Americans had
settled in western Tennessee, the area was the domain of a little
known native culture known as the Mound Builders. These
people left behind a fascinating network of enormous mounds,
many in the shapes of huge animals, over a vast area from
what's now the north central United States to the Gulf of Mexico,
and from the Mississippi River Valley to the Appalachian Mountains, including Robertson County, Tennessee.

There are a few mounds left, and they enjoy government
protection as historic sites. But most were destroyed by every-

thing from erosion and farmers to road builders and treasure hunters. The Mound Builders flourished from about 1000 to the mid 1500s, when they were pretty much done in by the Spanish. The Mound Builders are believed to have worshipped local gods and practiced human sacrifice.

One of the things the "Bell Witch's" 19th century fans would prod it to confess was its origin and purpose. What little they could ever get the parasites to tell had to do with Native American connections and a claim that they had been in the area for centuries. But with these critters' record for lying, who knows? Maybe the parasites themselves couldn't remember. Given the fluid nature of space and time in the multiverse, it isn't hard to understand the "witch's" apparent omniscience and bilocation. But if reports of its words and actions are accurate, the parasites exhibited a fascinating tendency I've noticed in other cases. The longer they spend attached to humans, or at least centered in our part of the multiverse, the more they seem to forget their own origins.

In any case the "Bell Witch" dissipated or departed within a year after the death of the elderly John Bell, whom I'm convinced "she" harassed to the point of harming his health, but didn't actually kill. "She" promised to return, and there have indeed been reports of occasional phenomena, real or imagined, that area. In early 2006 the producers of *An American Haunting* vowed to fly me to Tennessee to investigate this as part of a documentary video, but that hadn't happened as of this writing.

So it's my guess that the Bells and their townsmen were *entrées* for a clan of petty gods/goddesses who had seen better days.

The Art of the Fall

In adjoining galleries at the British Museum in London you can get a vivid picture of our descent into polytheism. In one gallery are the gods, goddesses, demons and monsters from after-the-fall cultures that generally were closer to the Earth and had to face the fickleness of life head-on, without the protections of what we call civilization.

It's understandable that people would develop images representing their fears as well as their joys. But looking upon the most ugly, petty and unlovable of these entities, I can't help but be convinced that parasites were in action somewhere along the line. That's especially true with the little tribal gods and backdoor deities that had to be satisfied with blood, with one horror or another. More often than not, they were honored by warlike peoples who undoubtedly "fed" these "gods" well. And in the scheme of things, they did far more dividing than uniting.

What people would deliberately choose such loveless gods? Only those who had been suckered into believing they had no choice.

In nearby galleries, however, there are some far more dignified and inspiring figures. In the Egyptian exhibit are the noble faces of Isis and her consort Osiris, Mother and Father of the world. From ancient Greece comes the graceful figure of Aphrodite, as carved 2,400 years ago by the sculptor Praxiteles. As though gazing from a temple in Asia is the serene face of the Buddha.

It's hard to believe that *these* deities represent "life-sucking ghosts." They bring us to the second part of our answer about how God became gods, and it's even stranger than what you've read so far.

6

Neutrals:
The Wrong One

God rises in the divine council,
He gives judgment in the midst of the gods.
"How long will you judge unjustly
and favor the cause of the wicked?
Defend the lowly and fatherless;
render justice to the afflicted and needy.
Rescue the lowly and poor;
deliver them from the hand of the wicked...."
I declare: "Gods though you be,
offspring of the Most High all of you,
Yet like any mortal you shall die;
like any prince you shall fall."
-Psalm 82

Mercifully there's more to the human race than ignorance, greed, lust and individualism. Deep inside we remember the Dream Time. We remember the Unity, and I like to think that there are only a few of us whom parasites have been able to "farm" into complete submission, or whose inborn faith they have totally hijacked.

Sometime before 6,000 years ago, and maybe as far back as a quarter-million years, somebody appears to have thrown a curve ball at both the parasites and us. There seem to have been different "outside influences." They probably were people – people from somewhere or somewhen else in the multiverse. It's these intruders who form part two of our answer about what happened to God and to us.

From Unlikely Sources

One of my prime rules as both a paranormal investigator and a journalist is never to take what I see and hear at face value. Things are seldom what they appear to be. The same can be applied to anthropology, archaeology and history. Nevertheless there are times when so many points of evidence come together, often from the most unlikely people and places, that we can't brush them off.

In 1968 a Swiss first-time author, Erich von Däniken (1935-) published a book called *Chariots of the Gods*. Building on the work of earlier writers and using circumstantial evidence, much of which was poorly researched, misinterpreted or even fraudulent, von Däniken tried to show that the ancient gods actually were based on tech-savvy space travelers from another planet. These prehistoric astronauts, von Däniken argued, wowed our ancestors into thinking they were gods and goddesses.

This is known today as the Paleocontact Theory.

Von Däniken, who has written twenty-six books and is still clicking, became an immediate lightning rod for attack by mainstream scientists. They would have ignored him, but *Chariots of the Gods* hit the best-seller lists without undue delay. Today there are an estimated sixty-five million von Däniken books in print, filled with pictures of ancient art in which beings look like they're flying through the air in vehicles, or wearing space suits. There have been numerous documentary and motion-picture derivatives.

Among the top criticisms of von Däniken's work, and that of others like him, is that any untrained eye can look at the symbolism of ancient art and see things in a modern context: machinery, aircraft and astronauts, for example. If I show you, say, a 15th century Inca carving with a figure in weird clothing handing a farmer a big box and a small disk, I could claim it's solid proof that aliens gave the Incas advanced dishwashing technology.

The von Däniken approach also includes the implication that our ancestors were too stupid to erect the Pyramids, the Easter Island statues or Stonehenge without the help of super-advanced UFO jockeys who, for reasons known only to the gods, liked to build things out of rocks.

Many barbs hurled at von Däniken are personal. Critics have derided him as an "innkeeper." Actually he was the managing director of a five-star hotel. He's a "self-appointed expert with a high school education." In fact, von Däniken studied comparative religion at the prestigious College St-Michel in Fribourg, Switzerland, founded in the 16th century. And they bring up his all-too-true conviction for embezzlement.

By contrast, Thomas Edison, whose scientific genius changed the daily lives of all of us forever, had a grand total of three months of formal schooling. Several of his teachers considered him a nitwit.

Criticism of von Däniken came even from the world-famous American astronomer, astrobiologist, popular-science guru and novelist Carl Sagan (1934-1996). While Sagan was a great believer in extraterrestrial life, and was even open to the possibility of some sort of paleocontact, he thought von Däniken's work was baloney. Bizarre as some of my own theories may seem, my opinion of von Däniken's work isn't far from Sagan's.

But despite his shortcomings, von Däniken brought to popular attention a crucial idea that has resonated with millions, and he has taught us that we must move outside ourselves and our very limited worldview. He showed us that we must, in early 21st century parlance, "think outside the box." Even though he may have botched the details and much of the evidence, von Däniken may be barking up the right tree.

After all, what is the professional archaeologist's "trained eye" trained to see? Things, and interpretations of newly discovered things, taught to it by its professors and by the authors of books it has read, which were in turn taught to them by earlier professors, and so on. While new and exciting discoveries are taking place in all sciences, archaeology not the least, the basic patterns we're trained to see in the art and technology of a given ancient culture arise from a framework that essentially was built on the worldview and attitudes of the 19th century.

While archaeologists today are giving more credit to ancient peoples for their intelligence and ingenuity, most artifacts we don't understand still are considered "ritual" in nature. The trained eye is not trained to see what it doesn't expect: evidence of the "outside influences" this book suggests.

I'm encouraged, however, by the recent trend known as the "processual approach." This takes archaeology away from the realm of history and nudges it toward anthropology. This ought to help bring to the fore the ancient peoples and their societies rather than their artifacts alone. By seeing artifacts more in the context of the people who produced them, the "trained eye" might develop a little peripheral vision for a change. But will this perspective be broad enough to allow objective consideration of truly unorthodox ideas?

The Genes that Shouldn't Be There

There are far more distinguished voices than von Däniken's being raised in the same direction as his.

Christian O'Brien (1908-1996), an industrial geologist, archaeologist and scholar of ancient languages, agreed that *somebody* very out of the ordinary influenced the civilizations and religions of the ancient world; mostly for the better, in his opinion.

Prolific author Zacharia Sitchin (1920-), who, like me, studied Hebrew so he could read the Bible's *Book of Genesis* in its original language, is convinced that alien visitors are responsible not only for legends of ancient gods, but for terrible wars and irresponsible manipulation of human genetics.

Looking at the Human Genome Project, completed in 2003, one wonders if the man doesn't have a point. One finding in particular raised many eyebrows, trained and otherwise. In this thirteen-year project to literally "map" all 25,000 genes in human DNA, and the three billion chemical pairs that compose it, researchers found a genuine mystery in the evolutionary record as revealed in human genes. It seems that human DNA contains 223 genes that shouldn't be there if evolution as we understand it is true. These genes don't have the required evolutionary forbears in the "family tree" of life on Earth.

So where did they come from?

For lack of any better answer, most mainstream biologists postulate some kind of "horizontal transfer from bacteria." Our old friend Sir Fred Hoyle would say that the genetic changes were "seeded" on Earth by cosmic "dust clouds" or passing comets. Others, like O'Brien and Sitchin, would assert that ancient astronauts deliberately did the transferring or the seeding.

With what I've seen in the realm of the paranormal, my viewpoint is somewhat different.

The idea that alien-laden spaceships would travel unimaginable distances through outer space to get to this backwater planet to manipulate, use, teach, harass or otherwise bother with us is questionable at best. But the genetic record, and our race memories as preserved in our myth and folklore, strongly suggest that something like that happened. But I doubt that whoever it was traveled from another planet in the same way that we travel in space.

I think instead that they quite literally dropped in from elsewhere and elsewhen in the multiverse. And I'm convinced that, unlike parasites, these intruders dropped in by accident. Nevertheless, they affected our race and our history in ways parasites never could.

Von Däniken, O'Brien, Sitchin and others essentially believe that these intruders came to Earth to establish a colony, genetically altering the pre-human species they found to make us into their own "image and likeness." Sitchin, who believes that they came from "Niburu," a nearby solar planet that later exploded and became the asteroid belt, is convinced that modern humans were intentionally created as slaves for these aliens.

When did all this supposedly happen? Believers generally place the beginnings of these goings-on between half a million and a quarter million years ago. That's interesting, since climate researchers say that the interglacial period of some 400,000 years ago closely matched our own climate era because the shape of the Earth's orbit was the same as it is now. That means that if dear old "intelligent life as we know it" existed, and had the capability of language, civilizations could exist too. Many civilizations.

All we know for sure is that something strange happened much more recently. About 6,000 years ago, the first known civilization sprang up, seemingly out of nowhere. We've already met the Sumerians, who started out worshipping one God. The weird thing is that their civilization appeared almost overnight.

What Happened?

That the multiverse is like Swiss cheese should be obvious from what we've seen of the paranormal so far. People we see as "ghosts" come and go and, apparently, they see *us* as ghosts from their own sides of countless world boundaries. Parasites, and who knows what other life forms, also come and go, many seemingly at random and without the intention of doing so.

I call them "drop-ins."

Where does Bigfoot, that giant man-ape known in various legends and forms around the planet, come from? Thousands of people have reported seeing specimens of Bigfoot but, as far as we know, nobody has ever caught one. All we have are hundreds of credible sightings (sometimes by multiple witnesses), humungous footprints, some (usually blurry) photographs, and a couple of hairs.

What about UFOs and supposed space aliens having "close encounters" with humans? In many of the countless stories, UFOs and/or the aliens themselves simply appear or disappear right in front of people. And there seem to be no end of UFO types or alien races coming and going.

Then there are the out-of-place, unknown or totally outrageous creatures that have no business being where there are, or even existing at all. Forget Wisconsin's unexplained kangaroo outbreak of the mid-20th century, the Loch Ness Monster or the Jersey Devil. Try explaining "Mothman" (as it was dubbed by the media), the headless, winged beast with glowing red eyes that chased cars while flying at 100 miles per hour. He, she or it terrorized America's Ohio River Valley in the 1960s.

How about the "Dover Demon," the well-attested critter seen over a three-day period in 1977 in that Massachusetts town, not twenty miles from where my family and I live today?

My files are full of documented cases like these from all over the world: people, animals, everyday objects, buildings, even whole towns that simply appear for awhile, then slip back to wherever or whenever they came from. Slips in time and space, little burps across the membranes of the multiverse: I've spoken with actual witnesses.

There are a few cases of dazed people who have appeared in international airports, speaking no known language, wearing clothes made from no known textiles, and carrying passports from countries that never existed. If they didn't disappear again, or have accidents in their terror and confusion, they usually ended up in psychiatric institutions.

And the people who disappear from our conscious world – where or when do they go? There are cases of people disappearing from one building and appearing in another. Others have disappeared from one continent and turned up – immediately – on another. Still others have vanished, then returned days later, believing that no time, or an inordinate amount of time, had elapsed.

Some vanish and are never seen again. Or are they?

Multiversal Tourists?

In the bed of the Paluxy River in Texas are some of the most jaw-dropping fossils I've ever seen. Intermixed are what appear to be dinosaur tracks and human footprints – impossible according to all accepted science because dinosaurs were extinct over 60 million years before humans came along. Other sites with what seem to be human-like footprints in impossibly ancient rock strata have been found in Kentucky, Illinois, and Central Asia.

In one fossil found in Utah in 1968, whatever made the footprint evidently was wearing a shoe or sandal while stepping on a trilobite, an ancestor of the horseshoe crab that lived some 500 million years ago! If these really are the tracks of some luckless, misplaced human, he or she wouldn't have lasted long: Earth's atmosphere at that period would have been toxic to us. Mainstream scientists, of course, either ignore or reject such fossils, and they often cite good scientific reasons for doing so. Maybe they're right. Or maybe they're succumbing to human nature. After all, if you had spent $50,000 to $100,000 on an advanced degree, would you appreciate someone without such a degree questioning what you'd worked so hard to learn?

Why are alleged photographs of ghosts, UFOs, Bigfoot and other multiverse "tourists" usually blurry? Because of those cross-world EMFs we've said so much about in previous chapters: They agitate the protons that make up the light picked up by the camera, whether using film or digital technology.

My point is that accounts of people, places and things that drop in and out of holes in the multiverse could fill volumes. As a matter of fact I believe that the same process is responsible for *all* things paranormal. Connect the dots, and they're all related. Connect the dots, and you'll see one picture: quantum physics and the multiverse as the root of all reality – the fingerprint of God on a Creation that is so varied, so vast and so alive that our shrunken modern minds are incapable of even beginning to grasp it.

I submit that the intruders who so influenced our known civilizations were drop-ins from a place or time whose technology was superior to that of whomever or whatever they found. Whoever they were, there seems to have been a large group of them. They apparently vanished from where and when they were, and reappeared – gear, vehicles and all – in the prehistoric world.

There are tantalizing archaeological clues that may or may not be evidence of these theoretical intruders, but they indicate to me that somebody taught our remote ancestors things they were very unlikely to learn on their own with the stone-age or bronze-age technology at their disposal.

From Europe and Central Asia there are several examples of aurochs, ancient bovines that fell into extinction about 6,000 years ago, that apparently were brought down by gunfire. More ominously there is a Neanderthal man's skull, found sixty feet below ground in what is now Zambia, in Africa, in 1921, that has clear entry and exit bullet wounds. One forensics expert told me the wounds look identical to those produced by today's high-velocity rifles. Neanderthals are believed to have been extinct by 28,000 years ago.

Somebody also dropped by with healing technology.

Among the many examples of impossibly ancient surgery and medicine deduced from human remains are the successful repair of a two-inch hole in the head of an Armenian woman some 4,000 years ago, root-canal and other extremely sophisticated dental work done on people in Pakistan some 9,000 years gone, and apparent open-heart surgery carried on in Central Asia some 5,000 years past.

Regardless of our opinion of von Däniken and his fellow paleocontact theorists, evidence is still evidence. The questions are, who was responsible, and what does it mean?

Perhaps our trusty tools myth and folklore can once again help clarify things.

The Elohim Enigma

בראשית ברא אלהים את השמים ואת הארץ

"Bereshith bara Elohim 'eth ha'shamayim w'eth ha'ares."

"In the beginning, God created the heavens and the Earth."

Genesis. The book of origins. Depending on whom you talk to, the Bible's first book was written as long ago as 5,500 years or as recently as 2,400 years. But nobody denies that it's one of the world's oldest accounts of human beginnings.

The trouble with all ancient scriptures (hand copies upon hand copies upon hand copies, with mistakes multiplying as they went) is compounded in the case of *Genesis* not only by the antiquity of the text but by its language. Hebrew, like other Semitic languages, has no written vowels. In modern Hebrew, at least, there are vowel marks. But in days of yore, the correct interpretation – even translation — of the written word depended entirely on what the speaker or writer meant, and what the reader believed.

How are we supposed to know that from a distance of over two millennia?

אלהים *Elohim*, the most ancient word for God used in *Genesis*, appears to date from the Bronze Age and, oddly, also was used to describe the whole group of gods worshipped by the Canaanites, the people who lived in Palestine before the Israelites arrived. *Elohim* is a genuine head-scratcher. A feminine noun with a masculine plural ending, there is no other word like it in Hebrew or any other Semitic language.

Depending on its context, it can mean "God" or "Gods." Literally translated, it means, "Those with the Shining Faces." It's the same word used by ancient people throughout the Middle East to describe a mysterious group of people known as "The Lords of Cultivation."

Between *Elohim* and two other ambiguous words in the Hebrew text, the first verse of *Genesis* could be translated, and has been by at least one ancient-language scholar, as something like: "When it started, Those with the Shining Faces looked down with pleasure upon the highland pastures and the lowland plains."

Genesis isn't the only creation account that has come down to us. Contemporary documents from neighboring Middle Eastern peoples include the seven *Kharsag Epics* of our friends, the Sumerians, and the *Atra-Hasis* of the Akkadians, rulers of the first known empire.

Put the *Atra-Hasis*, the *Kharsag Epics* and *Genesis* (with a slightly alternate translation) together, take out the divine imagery, and what you get is something very much like this:

Sometime before 6,000 years ago, a group of very unusual people suddenly arrived in the Middle East from parts unknown. They established an agricultural colony whose name has come down to us as Ehdin or Eden. From archaeological evidence of very early and large-scale construction, irrigation and agricultural activity there, this colony probably was centered in the fertile Qadisha Valley of Lebanon.

Fascinatingly, this area has been known from time out of mind as the "Holy Valley," and the incredibly ancient main town is known as Ehden. The very name Qadisha comes from the Semitic root word for "holiness." Pagans believed that the valley and the surrounding mountains had been home to gods. Later, Christian monks and even Muslim hermits of the Sufi sect came to the Holy Valley to live and pray.

In a thought-provoking lesson for our own times, medieval pilgrims to the area often reported how the Christians and Muslims helped each other, especially when it came to growing food. A shade or two of the Garden of Eden, as we've come to understand it?

In any case, the ancient super farmers had a chief ("the Most High") who lived either on a very high mountain or on an island in the sky, and was known variously as Anu, or El Shaddai. At the colony he had a governor or manager, known variously as Enlil, Kharsag or Yahweh. This governor had a wife or consort known as Ninlil, Ninkarsag or Shekinah.

The governor or manager supervised the agricultural work by his subordinates, known variously as the *Annunage* or the *Elohim*. In the texts, these beings clearly correspond with what we would call angels. Of particular importance was construction of a reservoir and irrigation canals at Ehden/Eden. The Most High's wife, meanwhile, comes across to modern eyes as nothing so much as a researcher of some kind, breeding various kinds of plants, and even animals.

The idea of a "Council of the Gods," headed by "The Most High" is present in all these documents. One reference that filtered down, and ended up in the Bible's *Book of Psalms,* opens this chapter. It has provided no end of fodder for arguments and rationalizations among Bible scholars.

After as little as forty years or as many as 3,600 (depending on the document), there was trouble in paradise. Whether because the whole frustrated group was stuck in that part of the multiverse and couldn't manage to get home, or simply because the *Annunage/Elohim* weren't spring chickens anymore, there appears to have been a violent labor strike. To resolve this, somebody suggested that the primitive humans around at the time be prepped as replacement workers.

"In the Image and Likeness of God"?

The *Atra-Hasis* almost literally describes a process of test-tube genetic engineering, in which Ninlil (whom the Akkadians considered the Mother Goddess) takes blood and saliva (two prime DNA sources) from one of the *Elohim* and engineers human beings as we know them. The Akkadians, by the way, called Ninlil "Mama." Have a familiar ring?

If it all really did happen this way…if we are what we are partly because of genetic manipulation by intruders from elsewhere and elsewhen in the multiverse, it would be the most significant discovery in human history. It would, in fact, *be* the discovery of human history.

The drama doesn't end here. Reading further in the texts and down the centuries, one encounters more worker rebellions, both by the humans and by the remaining *Annunage/Elohim.* A group of the latter broke some apparent non-fraternization rule, taking wives from among the new humans, who in *Genesis*

Part of the extensive Qadisha Valley in Lebanon.

have tremendous lifespans, up to nearly 1,000 years. These *liaisons* brought down the wrath of "The Most High." *Genesis* 6:1 describes how the *Nephilim* (either intruders themselves or half-breeds) "saw that the daughters of man were attractive. And they took as their wives any they chose."

For these infractions, Anu/El Shaddai barred humans from the now complete Ehden/Eden, and confined the most rebellious *Annunage/Elohim* to what sounds like the volcanic Rift

Valley, which stretches from southern Lebanon all the way to Kenya. In the *Book of Enoch*, which the Christian Church did not include in its Bible, that biblical forefather describes being taken for rides in an aircraft by two angels. Among other sights, he looks down and sees their rebellious comrades languishing in a "valley of fire."

If myth and folklore are the vessels of our race memory, here's our creation of man, Garden of Eden, fall of man, fallen angels and hell (complete with sulfur and poisonous volcanic fumes) – in a nutshell.

Enoch, by the way, met a very intriguing fate. A sort of pet of the *Elohim* and emissary between them and the natives, this father of the long-lived Methuselah and great-grandfather of Noah, "walked with God; and he was not, for God took him." *Genesis* 5:24. Enoch and the later Prophet Elijah were the only Old Testament figures to be permanently carried off in "fiery chariots."

Crucially, the *Genesis* text continues that the *Nephilim*, these mixed-blood supermen, and their descendants went on to become "the mighty men who were of old, the men of renown." Some of the better gods and heroes of the later ancients, like those of the Greeks and Romans, maybe?

In any event, "the Most High's" chain of command eventually petered out and, armed with superior agricultural know-how and considerable technology, the remaining population of *Annunage/Elohim* and the modern humans under their sway spread out from Ehden/Eden. The texts speak of individual gods founding the first known cities of the ancient Middle East: Jericho, Ur, Uruk, Eridu, Lagash, Ebla, Baalbek, Nippur, and a few others, most named after the founding gods themselves.

All this took place about the time that civilization sprang up, seemingly out of nowhere, in the "Fertile Crescent" of present-day Iraq. This included sophisticated governments; law codes and civil services; highly developed religions centered, of course, around the city's founding god; businesses, and social institutions such as schools and hospitals.

As we've already noted, it's difficult to exaggerate how quickly this happened. It's as though the natives were bean farmers one month, and the next they were lawyers, architects and accountants, building huge cities, and suddenly worshipping a shipload of gods.

It's also difficult to exaggerate the reach of these extra-dimensional intruders, if that's what they were. If the worldwide tapestry of folklore is any guide, their influence was global. That could be one explanation for so many commonalities in myth, symbol and even religious architecture all over the planet, among cultures that supposedly had no contact with one another until the 18th or 19th centuries.

Why did the intruders and their "children" found cities? Certainly it was to support what was apparently a large population that now had a hankering (because of the new genes?) for more than just scraping a living in the desert. Could living in walled cities also have been to defend themselves against the violent and more primitive tribes and villages dominated by those other "gods" – the parasites?

And what happened to Ehden/Eden? Had it served its purpose? Was it overrun by primitive, parasite-worshipping humans? If all this did center in the Qadisha Valley, then Ehden is still there!

No matter what the answers, further reading in the ancient texts makes it clear that these *Annunage/Elohim* and/or their descendants knew they had a good thing going. They were literally worshipped by thousands, were wined and dined by armies of priests, and all they had to do was be bosses. Several later ancient texts describe these beings flying around in their own craft, overseeing their domains from the air, and sometimes taking junkets to other cities to hobnob with their "divine" counterparts.

Wars of the Gods

Unfortunately there was a dark side, and it also appears to have been global.

Like us, these "gods" were never quite satisfied with what they had. The ancient texts – not just the ones we've mentioned, but documents from cultures all over the world – indicate that the first organized wars between these new civilizations were orchestrated, and even physically led, by the "gods," who used not only their technology but their subject peoples to fight one another over control of an area, or perhaps even the whole planet.

Every single document speaks of flying vehicles and horrific weapons that laid waste vast territories. In the Bible alone, there are some 360 verses describing some sort of flying vehicle, whether ascending, descending, hovering or just flying, sometimes at amazing speeds.

Exodus 14:19-20 contains only one example.

"And the Angel of God, which went before the camp of Israel, removed and went behind them; and the pillar of the cloud went from before their face, and stood behind them. And it came between the camp of the Egyptians and the camp of Israel; and it was a cloud and darkness to them, but it gave light by night to these, so that the one came not near the other all the night."

The Hindu *Mahabharata* took its current form some 1,600 years ago. It is the "Epic of India" and the longest poem in the world. In what could have been the same, or an entirely different, intrusion from another part of the multiverse, the *Mahabharata* describes in gory detail a war among the gods as fought with aircraft called "vimana," air-to-air missiles, and what sounds hideously like nuclear weapons. Each major god had his or her own weapon, called an "astra," which used the power of the element it was based on. Agniastras, for example, wielded a "fire astra." For Suryaastra it was a "sun astra." And Varunasutra used a "water astra."

Descriptions of what the worst astras were capable of make the blood run cold.

The Narayanaastra was a thought-seeking missile – something still on the drawing board with our modern military gurus. It was directed against anything that was *adharma* (unrighteous). The great hero Krishna, however, was able to "absorb" the weapon's affects to protect others against instant death. Even nastier was the Brahmastra, used only in the most extreme need. It was based on "the power of the universe," could obliterate whole cities, and was the most horrific weapon in the intruders' arsenal. It takes genuine talent to explain this away as anything but a nuclear weapon.

From Book 7 of the *Mahabharata*:

"Gurkha, flying a swift and powerful vimana, hurled a single projectile charged with the power of the universe. An incandescent column of smoke and flame, as bright as ten thousand suns, rose with all its splendor...."It was an unknown weapon, an iron thunderbolt, a gigantic messenger of death, which reduced to ashes the entire race of the Vrishnis and the Andhakas....

"The corpses were so burned as to be unrecognizable. Hair and nails fell out; Pottery broke without apparent cause, and the birds turned white....

"...After a few hours all food was infected....Fierce winds began to blow upward, showering dust and gravel....The Earth shook, scorched by the terrible, violent heat of this weapon...."

How or why would ancient peoples make up stories like this in such detail? But hold on! Wouldn't there be archaeological evidence of such a terrible war, even in the distant past? There is.

In areas from the Middle East (including Epypt) through India, there have been finds of ancient desert sand fused into greenish glass – something that happens only at "ground zero" of a nuclear blast.

When the ancient, once-flourishing Indus Valley city the locals called Mohenjo Daro, in southern Pakistan, was first excavated in the early years of the last century, archaeologists were perplexed at nearly everything they found. There was evidence of quick abandonment of the city, which prospered between 2600 and 1900 B.C. The relatively few skeletons found were in an oddly burned state, and there were signs that some buildings had literally melted. There was even a circular "ground zero," where the whole area had been leveled.

During one of the excavations some years later, somebody brought a Geiger counter. They found that the whole vicinity was radioactive far beyond what would have occurred naturally, and that the skeletons were some fifty times more radioactive than normal. The sand had been heat-fused into greenish glass.

Mohenjo Daro means "Mound of the Dead."

The Lawgivers

While precisely when they were here is uncertain, these intruders had such a deep affect on our species that we remember them today not only in our myth and folklore, but even in our modern institutions, religions, and in our very languages.

When Hammurabi ("The Lawgiver") ascended the throne of Babylon in 1792 B.C., he not only set out to unite the old Sumerian and Akkadian realms into the new Babylonian Empire, he proclaimed the first known law code, in 282 articles. Right in the Prologue, Hammurabi claims that he's basing the Code on the decrees by which Anu and Enlil had governed the *Annunage/Elohim.*

The ruins of the ancient city of Mohenjo Daro in southern Pakistan. Some maverick researchers believe the city was destroyed in a nuclear blast.

The Code of Hammurabi is a little rough *vis a vis* the death penalty, and it condones slavery, but it has many seeds of justice that echo through our laws even today, including fairness for people of all classes, and even equality for women under the law.

The ancients generally thought of the intruders as coming from the mountains or the sky. They're certainly remembered as avid aviators. In most religions even today, we think of God as living in the sky. Heaven is always "up there," God is "the Man up there," and hell is somewhere within the Earth. In the New Testament, Jesus ascends into heaven (*Luke* 24:50-51, *Acts of the Apostles* 1:9). In *Acts*, the apostles even "lost sight of Him in a cloud." When we die, we head for that great law court, golf course, bowling alley or whatever "in the sky."

The Indo-European language group includes several hundred languages and dialects — almost all the tongues spoken from Europe eastward and southward through the Middle East to the northern half of India. Nearly half the world's population speaks an Indo-European language, either as a native tongue or a business language. The languages include English, and they apparently descend from a common language once spoken throughout that region. Many words are similar from language to language. The first words nearly all of us say, "mama" and "papa," are the same or similar in all Indo-European languages...just as with the Akkadians when they referred to Ninlil, the Mother Goddess.

We could go on and on. The point is that the arrival and activity of these intruders, whoever they were, wherever or whenever they came from, is probably the most well documented occurrence in human prehistory. It was global in scope, it changed our species forever, and I believe it happened not because of ancient space travelers, but because of people – albeit a different kind of people – falling through, being pulled through, or deliberately traversing world boundaries in the multiverse.

Who knows how many times these intrusions took place in the vast, dark millennia of human prehistory? Whether it happened once or twenty times, our first reaction may be that these intruders made the parasites of our last chapter look like amateurs when it came to messing with us.

If they really did blend their DNA with ours, what did they give us and what did they take away? Didn't they drag us even further from our Primal God than the parasites already had? Didn't they further fragment us? By preying on our fear and ignorance in their selfishness and greed, and by pretending to be gods, didn't they push us even further from the Unity?

Maybe and maybe not.

I've called them "intruders" because there's documentary evidence that some of them used us as pawns in their wars with each other, and because those wars did tremendous damage, possibly incinerating whole cities, regions and peoples. But it can be argued that the best of these drop-ins did some good. If they really did bring healing and benign technology, that can hardly be called evil. It also can be argued that they gave us civilization, though they perhaps lost it along with us because of their wars.

But who were they? If they really did share their DNA with us, they couldn't have been all that different. "Those with the Shining Faces" couldn't have been all that alien, even though their technology certainly seemed that way to our ancestors.

If they felt the need to change us genetically, what were we like before that? Did they make us fully human by making us like themselves? Weren't they, like us, prey for parasites? And, perhaps most intriguingly, are their descendants among us today? If so, at this distance in time from their interaction, certainly everyone alive would share those genes. From what little we know of them, the intruders were capable of great good and great evil, great love and great hatred. They embodied the best and the worst.

Just like us.

Maybe the intruders didn't drive us further from our Primal God. Perhaps by giving us universal father and mother figures that stuck in our minds, and perhaps even in our DNA, the intruders inadvertently threw us a lifeline that eventually helped us begin reconnecting with our Primal God, who was seen by our most remote, pre-intruder ancestors as Father and Mother. Whether called Yahweh and Shekinah, Enlil and Ninlil, or Kharsag and Ninkharsag, the king and queen of that primeval agricultural colony, if that's what it was, may have offered a re-linking to something very deep in our common being.

In earlier chapters I tried to get across that to understand God, ourselves and our destiny we must accept and understand the paranormal, because the paranormal is the conduit through which we experience everything. It's the maze we pass through as we traverse life. And we never know who or what we'll meet! If the paranormal, and the vagaries of the multiverse, are so pervasive, have there been other organized visitations, as opposed to accidental drop-ins, by groups of intruders?

I believe not only that there have been, but that they take place frequently.

In the Shadow of Mothman

What our ancestors saw as guardian "pillars of flame" or dog-fighting "vimanas," we would today call UFOs.

What few press reports mentioned during the Mothman incidents of the 1960s in Ohio and West Virginia were that these were accompanied by nightly sightings of strange lights in the sky, along with an upsurge in ghost reports, especially poltergeist activity. It was what paranormal investigators call a "flap": an outbreak of bizarre but seemingly unrelated paranormal activity. I believe it happens when several quite different parallel worlds temporarily overlap over a large physical area. It's not an unusual occurrence, and it can last for years.

Author and journalist John A. Keel (1930-), who wrote *The Mothman Prophecies,* and is one of the few who's been at this longer than I have, documented the Ohio Valley flap of the

1960s in great detail. Among the oddities were first-hand reports of strange-looking people who would turn up on local doorsteps, claim they were from the Air Force or some other government agency, then grill the residents about what paranormal events they had experienced.

Those grilled reported that many interviewers spoke as though they weren't used to English or to dealing with simple niceties like shaking hands. Military veterans noted that alleged Air Force representatives sometimes wore their uniforms incorrectly, had insignia in the wrong places, or had made other mistakes in dress. Sometimes the visitors said they were from government agencies the interviewees later found to be nonexistent.

Reported occurrences I find especially fascinating during this flap include these inexplicable visitors asking to keep simple items like ball-point pens or ashtrays. When given these items, they would walk away enthralled, as though they had a mint-condition antique or rare artifact.

Keel's beliefs are similar to mine. Paranormal events never take place in isolation. Like everything in the multiverse, they are intimately connected with each other, with us and with every other denizen.

I'm convinced that the intruders and other events darkly mirrored in the *Atra-Hasis*, the *Kharsag Epics*, *Genesis*, the *Mahabharata* and other ancient texts don't stand in isolation from thousands of other intrusions across the countless boundaries of countless worlds. Whether they be parasites or people like – or almost like – us, they usually don't seem to be any great friends of ours.

Is There a Devil?

We can't close any discussion about paranormal enemies – or possible enemies — without dealing with a question I hear very frequently: Does the Devil exist?

Whether you call him Satan, as Jews and Christians do; Iblis as do Muslims; or Mainyu as do Zoroastrians, belief in a single being who personifies evil, or at least runs the horror show, is on the rise today. And why not? Nobody who watches television or reads the newspaper can ignore the presence of evil in the world.

There's plenty of reason to believe in a devil. After all, look what parasites and intruders have done to our species, or nudged us into doing to ourselves. Pinning a name and focusing blame always make problems easier to grasp, and maybe even easier to deal with. If we have a chief devil to blame for evil, maybe that eases our personal responsibility to try and stop it.

There's deep irony in the question of the Devil's existence. And there's at least one answer that has a deeper irony. From a certain point of view, and I'm sorry if this is offensive to any reader, one could argue that the person at the top in that theoretical agricultural colony in the deeps of time was the origin of our concept of the Devil. Whether you call him Enlil, Kharsag, Yahweh or something else, he was, according to one text or another, responsible not only for dividing humans from our Primal God and each other, but for repeated genocide, mass slavery, environmental devastation, and one global bloodbath after another.

You could pin the same crimes on us as a species, so I think the mirror is the best place to look for the Devil. Of all today's religions, I think the Wiccans (a group of neopagans devoted to the Earth) are among the few to get it right. They don't believe in a personal Devil. They believe that people are responsible for their own actions, and for the consequences that follow.

Very fortunately, and despite the enemies, the evil, and intruders who may not care one way or the other, we have friends in the multiverse too. And the identity and utter power of some of them may surprise you.

7

Friends: Guides and Guardians

For an angel of peace,
A faithful guide and guardian of our souls and bodies,
Let us ask of the Lord.
-From the Eastern Orthodox Divine Liturgy

Everyone in the military who has half a chance of serving in a forward area undergoes some tough survival training. Part of mine took place during a hideous January week in the Saint Elias Mountains of Canada's Yukon Territory. Landing in a valley, we proceeded to literally burrow into the snow, hollowing out small caves where we were to live for the ensuing five days.

We had plenty of incentive: The wind-chill factor was -85 F!

Having survived the night, mole-like in our burrows (which can be surprisingly comfortable if you know what you're doing), several of us had to do a mock reconnaissance sortie. Setting out on snowshoes, and complete with packs and radio gear, we headed for a nearby ridge. As we rounded a corner, there was a tremendous blast of wind, and what must have been a ton of snow on an outcropping above us gave way. It came down right on top of you-know-who. I vanished under this small avalanche as my companions shouted in terror. Then all was darkness and silence. I was on my back, and the pressure on every inch of my body was unbearable.

I couldn't breathe, and I had a certainty that I was going to die.

Just as panic set in, my attention was wrenched toward my right hand. I felt a tingle, then what I can only describe as a warm touch. It felt like someone was taking my hand *right through the thick, down glove.*

Someone did. Someone took my hand and literally pulled me up through some eight feet of snow. All I remember is feeling my right hand break free of the snow, then being grabbed, dug out and pulled by one of the other men. I was back in the blessed air amid my astounded companions!

They had begun frantically digging for me as soon as the mini-avalanche occurred. The one who pulled me free said that my hand had simply popped up right in front of him as he dug. They couldn't fathom how I'd gotten from the bottom of the small mountain of snow to a point where my arm was visible!

To add to their astonishment, especially that of the medical corpsman, I didn't have a scratch. No broken bones, no abrasions, not even a bruise. As a matter of fact, while some of the Canadians in the contingent were later carted off to the base in Whitehorse with hypothermia, "The Yank," as they called me, made it through the whole week!

More Angels than Parasites

Unseen lifesavers, angels, guardian spirits, comforting presences, spirit guides: Belief in some sort of spiritual helpers and their action among humans is just as present in our race memories – and in our daily lives — as that of parasites and intruders…probably more so.

Angel comes from the Greek word   αγγελος (*angelos*), meaning messenger. Archangel (like the Archangel Michael) simply means chief messenger. Belief in angels is basic to Judaism and Christianity, and it's one of the "Six Pillars of Belief" in Muhammedanism. Mormons claim that their whole faith began with a message from an angel. Devas are among the spiritual beings Hindus and Buddhists rely on for help.

Can you guess how devas translates? "Those with the Shining Faces!"

Angels as we know them don't turn up in sacred texts until after we begin emerging from deepest, darkest antiquity. Perhaps the more negative of the ancient intruders eventually got back to wherever or whenever they came from, died out, lost interest in our usefulness, or simply were absorbed into the human population over the centuries. After that, perhaps more positive entities grabbed our attention more often, or actively tried to help us as, in the wake of the intruders, our societies became more complex, our wars more deadly, and our religions more confusing and less satisfying.

Whatever the answer, the later the texts, the more positive these entities tend to seem. In the western world today, in fact, angels and their action among us are popular subjects. While people in the 21st century still kill each other in the name of God, just about everyone from most any religious background can relate to angels. That's probably because we haven't piled the complex doctrinal and sectarian baggage on angels that we've piled on God.

Nearly everyone has a story about a close call or an impossible escape in which we *knew* that someone or something beyond ourselves was giving us help. In some cases the experience was life-transforming. In other cases it was life-saving. In my case it was both. Either way, we're never the same again. But no matter what name your religion gives them, who or what are these helpers?

There are plenty of popular books that try to answer that question, many of them dripping with sap and written by people with little spiritual training or folklore-studies background. So what do our trusty memory-vessels, myth and folklore, have to say?

Certainly some of the most fascinating clues to the later manifestations of benign beings from other parts of the multiverse comes from the Bible. There, as we saw early on in the *Book of Genesis*, the Hebrew word *Elohim* was used interchangeably to mean God, God and His angels, or just the angels. In our last chapter we interpreted many of these *Elohim* as the houseguests from hell: Intruders from elsewhere and elsewhen who interfered in human history, and perhaps even manipulated our genes.

But as our race memory emerges from the depths of prehistory, not only are there more indications of benign entities, there are hints that our ancestors may have been reconnecting at last with our Primal God with their help. It's almost as if some of these new guardians, whoever or whatever they were, tried to undo part of the damage parasites and intruders had done.

The Sacred Tetragrammaton

Traditionally, *Genesis* was written by Moses. But biblical scholars today talk about the "P," "J," and "E" authors, depending on what style a given section is written in, and what word is used for God. The "P" and "E" writers tended to use *Elohim*, and the later "J" sticks with Yahweh or Jehovah, made-up words based on the "Sacred Tetragrammaton," the four known letters of the secret Name of God: יְהֹוָה, transliterated as YHWH or JHVH.

By the time the *Genesis* authors were talking about their forefather Abraham, who probably lived about 4,000 years ago, the Name represented by the Tetragrammaton had become so holy that people weren't allowed to say it. So when we get to *Genesis* Chapter 18 (the Sodom and Gomorrah story), we find YHWH with vowel marks, and pronounced by the substitute title "Adonai."

Like *Elohim*, however, this still seems to mean more than just God.

"And Adonai appeared to him (Abraham) by the oaks of Mamre as he sat in the tent door in the heat of the day. And he raised his eyes and looked. And lo! Three men stood by him; and when he saw Them he ran to meet Them from the tent door, and bowed himself to the ground, and said, 'My Lord, if now I have found favor in Your sight, pass not away, I pray You, from Your servant.'"

Adonai, all three of Him, then sat at a table and ate a large meal prepared by Sara, Abraham's wife. Afterward, Adonai predicted that the couple would have a child, even though they were elderly. The child turned out to be Isaac, considered the father of the Hebrew nation.

This sounds like a typical story of the intruders we met in the last chapter, especially because two of them continued down the road, proceeding to fry Sodom and Gomorrah in another attack that sounds suspiciously nuclear. But there appears to be a transition going on here: a reconnection between humans and a more spiritual God. We're beginning to meet angels who aren't agricultural drones or rebels who lust after human women, but powerful, focused agents of the will of a God Who appreciates humans for their own sake.

"For I know him (Abraham), that he will command his household and his children after him, and they shall keep the way of the Lord, to do justice and judgment...."

Christian theologians see these three figures who appeared to Abraham as a foreshadowing of their doctrine of the Holy Trinity – Father, Son and Holy Spirit in one God. I find that very significant, since our Primal God, as you may remember, appears to have been three also – Father, Mother and Child (the child being either an actual offspring or us). By the time Christianity came along, the Trinity was an old idea.

Many Christian scholars have been bothered, however, by the dissimilarity between the vengeful, jealous God of the Hebrew Bible (the Old Testament) and the loving, forgiving God of their own New Testament. A few have said that it isn't even the same God. Given the evolution of religion as we've been tracing it in this book, they may be right. We may finally be moving beyond our theoretical, inter-dimensional warlords, Enlil, Kharsag and Yahweh, and getting hints of the God we originally knew.

As God became more loving, so did angels.

Maryam's Encounter

Muhammedanism is much younger than Judaism and postdates even Christianity. Muslims believe that revelations were given to the Prophet Muhammed for a little over twenty years, from roughly 610 to his death in 632. Teachings were passed on orally for about forty-three years after that, then were written down, eventually resulting in the Qur'an we know today. That makes it a very recent document compared with the others we've dealt with, and it sheds light on the more recent development of our understanding of angels (called in the Qur'an "Malaikah" or "those who are made from light") as positive beings.

Believe it or not, the Archangel Gabriel announces the birth of

Jesus to Mary not only in the New Testament but also in the Qur'an. In the Qur'an's *Sura Maryam*, Malaikah Jibril, the Muslim name for the Archangel Gabriel, appears to Maryam (Mary) "in the form of a handsome man."

"Then We (Allah) sent Our Spirit to her, and it took on for her the form of a handsome, well-built man. She said, 'I seek refuge from you with the All-Merciful if you guard against evil.' He said, 'I am only your Lord's messenger so that He can give you a pure boy.'" (*Sura Maryam* 16-19)

This certainly shows us a benign angel doing God's bidding for the good of humanity. But how can one ignore the suggestion here that infuriates many Christian theologians and believers alike? Was this a repeat of what the most ancient manuscripts said was the "crime" of the *Elohim*: "knowing" the daughters of men and having children by them? In Christian and Muslim belief, there is no doubt that Mary was inseminated in order to give birth to Jesus ("Issa" in the Qu'ran), whom Christians teach was "begotten of the Father." But Christians believe it was done without sexual intercourse – that Jesus was "born of a virgin" — a very important doctrine for them,.

Orthodox Christian teaching says much more: Not only did Mary remain a virgin, but Jesus, as fully God and fully Man, was "pre-existent." As God the Son, part of the Holy Trinity, He existed at the beginning of time and was the One through whom the universe was created.

How could He be the Creator and still be born as a man in the Middle East – begotten through an angel who is virtually equated with God? The only way to explain it would be the paranormal, and its "engine," quantum physics: In the multiverse, time and space have no objective meaning across the worlds. Things can and do take place before whatever caused them. Christ can exist before being born. But so can the rest of us.

The Message is in the Miracles

Once again we begin to see hints of the most mighty of concepts, known to our most distant ancestors, tricked away from us by parasites and stolen from us, however inadvertently, by the intruders. In fits and starts, we begin to see a glimpse of the Unity.

For example, the presence of angels in ancient texts usually is a signal that something miraculous is going to happen. Our word "miracle" comes from the Latin "miraculum," which means "something wonderful." Before that it's considered traceable to the Indo-European root "smei-," meaning "smile" or "laugh." Apparently miracles are supposed to make us happy, and that's not too long a leap for the imagination. But as usual, there's more.

In some theologies, and I think this is expressed most perfectly in that of Eastern Orthodox Christianity, miracles aren't considered special supernatural events. They're considered *restorations of the world as it is supposed to be.* In a world restored to the divine image in which it was originally created, miracles are the norm rather than the exception, the Orthodox believe. It's sickness, sorrow, evil and death that are out of the ordinary.

It's not much of a jump to the same idea in our own terms: In our Primal God, in the Unity, the Dream Time is restored, the negative is overwhelmed by the positive, lies are banished, love triumphs.

Angels certainly seem to bring the message of miracles. But just as we saw in Chapter 3, the story of what people believe, and why they believe it, goes far beyond official religious teaching. We gladly accept benign angels not because we are told to, and not just because their existence is a comforting thought, but because so many of us have experienced them for ourselves.

In my own experience as a paranormal investigator, there are many species of guardians (whatever you call them) just as there are many species of parasites. I suspect that, as with parasites, each species originates in a different world, and their theology isn't necessarily the same as ours. Do some or all of them "work for" our Primal God? Insofar as anyone in the multiverse strives to encourage life, love, and to restore the Unity, of course they do.

Miraculous healings, impossible escapes, "messages from beyond," uncanny good luck...these often are attributed to angels or other guardians from elsewhere in the multiverse. Taken to its logical conclusion, that means that if we ourselves have enough love, we can be guardians too, whether in our own world or beyond. We'll see just how real that can be in our final chapter.

Volunteers from Beyond

Beyond angels there are "spirit guides" and "guardian spirits" present in the beliefs of virtually every tradition of the planet.

Each tribal shaman has any number of entities he or she believes act as guide to and through other worlds in the quest for answers and cures. Most mediums claim there are spirits who act as guides and facilitators in the quest to link loved ones with those "beyond the veil."

While I suspect that at least a few of these "spirits" are parasites in camouflage, there certainly seem to be beings from elsewhere and elsewhen who take an interest in us in a very generous way. Indeed, there seem to be many worlds in which there is a greater awareness of the Unity than there is here, whose denizens (probably just as physical as we are) are more enlightened, and less self-centered, and who try to reach out and help whomever they can in the multiverse.

I suppose it's not unlike us helping strangers by volunteering at soup kitchens or putting in time on a Red Cross disaster-relief team.

because of their "higher awareness," or whatever you'd care to call it, these beings know, accept and use the multiverse, so they can see farther and know more than us, who huddle in our narrow and arrogant little world. To some degree they can manipulate space and time just as parasites do, though for far loftier reasons.

Whoever they are, they care. And I, for one, am darn glad of it. Whoever or whatever hauled me out of that Yukon snow mound so many years ago, thanks!

Unexpected Neighbors

We met some modern "neutral drop-ins" from the multiverse in the last chapter, but there are plenty of these from folklore too. And many of them seem just as frightened or confused by us as we are by them. Folklore is full of legends of beings that we have dubbed nature spirits, fairies, jinns, dryads, elves, leprechauns, and any number of other names. They are known in one form or another throughout the world and, while human experience with angels and other guardians is much more widespread, there are millennia full of stories about these other creatures as well. While some cultures attribute evil to a few races on this list, most are considered good-hearted, if not actual helpers, if we're in a pinch.

Some encounters with these fellow denizens of the multiverse are even stranger than you might expect, and the experiences run from ancient times to today.

Not all fairies in folklore are tiny people with little wings. Many sound just like some of the drop-ins we've talked about: indistinguishable from ordinary people, but of a different species entirely. I could fill this book with accounts of "out of thin air" appearances by non-angels and beings that our old myths might call fairies and our new ones "UFOnauts."

There were the "Green Children" of Europe, recorded from

the 12ᵗʰ through the 18ᵗʰ centuries. The "goblins" of Hopkinsville, Kentucky, turned up in 1955. A "tiny man" who left trails of miniscule footprints visited Dunn, North Carolina, in the 1970s. The "Magonians" and their "cloud ships" were reported over Europe off and on for centuries.

In my own work I've run into families in several different countries who absolutely insist that fairies (or the local equivalent) do their housework! In 1984, the parents of a family of five in Puerto Rico told me they left their home for a few hours every Saturday, even if it was just to take a long walk. In their kitchen they left behind some fruit and beer. When they got back, they claimed, all the housework was done, including the breakfast dishes!

I've heard similar stories while doing research in the United States, Britain, Canada and the South Pacific.

Whenever I've tried to set up cameras or recording equipment to see what really happened in a family's absence, *nothing* happened. And I got the blame for the housework not being done! Whatever multiversal welfare system is at work here, Jackie and I wouldn't mind hosting a few of these handy little "fairies" at *Maison Eno*. But so far, no luck.

Then there is the ubiquitous modern UFO, prominent throughout human history, but especially well known in North America and around the globe since the end of World War II. "Flying saucers" and people from other planets have been the staples of modern mythology. I believe the ones that can't be explained in any other way are visitors – mostly involuntary and mostly unconcerned with us – from other parts of that Swiss-cheese reality we call the multiverse.

Garden of Ehden/Eden Revisited?

Along with direct help rendered to us, deliberate attempts at mass communication sometimes are attributed to beings from places and times unknown. Probably the best examples of this in modern times are "crop circles," designs made in fields by someone or something that pushes the plants to the ground in an apparently ordered pattern, sometimes geometrically complex and extremely beautiful.

Many crop circles are celebrated hoaxes, and there's a British organization, Circlemakers, for those who enjoy creating crop circles and hope to expand their use as art forms. On the other hand there are circles that appear overnight with no known explanation. These have been reported all over the world. Odd phenomena, such as balls of light and shiny disks, sometimes are seen in the area before or after an anomalous crop circle appears.

Speculation is rife. Little-understood weather phenomena, such as microbursts, sometimes get the credit. Others, including me, lean toward a biophysical explanation: crop circles could be formed by electromagnetic phenomena known as "plasma vortices" that could bend the plants and create some of the same physical changes in them that researchers have documented. With all the electropollution in the atmosphere these days, heaven knows this phenomenon isn't unlikely.

But it's difficult to get past the obviously intelligent nature of most of these crop circles. Regardless of the process by which they're created, and Chaos Theory notwithstanding, can crop circles *not* have an intelligent designer? Discussing crop-circle creation is a fractal of discussing Creation itself: How could it all happen by chance?

In the end, many believe crop circles to be communications from beings they usually interpret as space aliens, though what the message is, nobody is sure.

Ancestors and Loved Ones

By far the most common friends I've run into in paranormal

research are people's ancestors – anyone from your "departed" mom to a distant forbear you may know nothing about.

When I talk about ancestors to an audience of European descent, I have to explain at length because ancestors simply aren't a big part of western spirituality. We may research our "roots" to see where we came from, but our interest usually stops at, "Did she wear a crown?" or "Did he invent the *pina colada?*" or especially, "Did they have bucks?"

People who descend from Eastern Hemisphere cultures, however, tend to know exactly what I'm talking about. They look at time differently. Their thinking spans not this year or the next, but centuries both behind them and before them. Their traditions include knowing and revering their ancestors.

Few of us realize it, but ancestors are among the most powerful guardians we have. If it hasn't happened to you, it's happened to people you know: The apparition of a departed loved one at the foot of the bed, the unmistakable feeling of his or her presence, even the smell of his pipe smoke or her perfume.

Skeptics tell us that our minds create the illusions of these things to help ease the pain of the passing. Certainly the more we love certain people, the more we miss them, and the more likely we'll find ways to compensate for their loss. But while our eyes and ears may lie, cameras, recording devices and multiple witnesses don't. Decades of paranormal research have filled my files with photographs, multiple-eyewitness accounts, and even a few apparent audio recordings (knowns as "electronic voice phenomena" or EVPS) of loved ones, usually in the act of being guardians – helping to protect and nurture their families.

Sometimes we feel the protecting presence of one whose identity we can't quite put a finger on, but whom we know we have a connection with.

I've documented cases of loved ones – sometimes loved ones

who were apparently distant ancestors not even known to family members – doing battle with parasites who were feeding off their descendants. I've seen departed loved ones taking concrete action to protect children from physical danger, even to the point of preventing accidents. I have numerous cases in which loved ones seem to have used dreams to warn people against danger or to give needed advice.

I've even seen unborn children – including one of my own – protect their families.

Taking the whole concept of life in the multiverse one more critical step, we can say this: Because there are worlds in which you are already enlightened and able to be a guardian, the guardian or one of the guardians you feel in your life *could be yourself lending you a hand from some close parallel world.* You could be your own guardian angel!

What can it mean for our conception of death and for our own ultimate destiny?

Human Destiny

8

Death and Life

How he lies in his rights of a man!
Death has done all Death can.
And absorbed in the new life he leads,
He recks not, he heeds
Nor his wrong nor my vengeance; both strike
On his senses alike,
And are lost in the solemn and strange
Surprise of the change.
-Robert Browning, *English Poet*

You've arrived at the most dangerous chapter in this book. That's because of what the paranormal has to tell us about our own lives and our own deaths.

On May 7, 2002, one Luke J. Helder, a junior at the University of Wisconsin, was arrested by the FBI and charged with planting a total of eighteen pipe bombs in mailboxes all over the American heartland. Six people were injured, and more bombs were found in Iowa, Illinois, Nebraska, Colorado and Texas. The twenty-one year-old Helder, armed with a shotgun, was arrested in Reno, Nevada, after a high-speed car chase. He told police that he relished the attention his actions brought, and his statements and writings indicated that he wasn't a Muslim terrorist or an anti-government crusader.

Instead, he was motivated by his devotion to New Age philosophy and the paranormal.

In a six-page letter to the university newspaper, Helder outlined his paranormal beliefs, the most notable being that death isn't real. He claimed that, along with the attention it brought him, his motivation as a bomber came from a desire to "enlighten the world" about his New Age thinking.

"I'm doing this because I care.... In the end you will know I was telling you the truth.... I'm taking very drastic measures in an attempt to provide this information to you."

Helder also espoused the New Age concept that each person can create his or her own reality.

"Once you begin to realize the potential you have as a consciousness/soul/spirit, you will begin to harness the abilities you have to produce realities.... You are not confined to the laws of physics.... Whether it's logic, meditation, channeling, astral projection, or ghosts, all are ways of knowing."

On ghosts, Helder wrote, "Many consciousnesses linger around on earth, clutching to material things; this is what ghosts are.... You may hear ghost stories, but have you ever seen one? If you haven't, get out the camera and start seeing.... I was curious about the existence of ghosts, and my curiosity led me to further investigation, which in turn allowed me to know ghosts truly do exist. Needless to say, it was an exciting occasion to finally see one! When I got my film developed to find orbs, the week was even more exciting!"

Helder's attitude is scary enough. But for me, who has asked the same questions and, I like to think, answered at least some of them, Helder's conclusions, and his actions in response to them, are positively chilling. I certainly reject Helder's sociopathic actions, his 19th century "retro" idea of what ghosts are, and his dubious assumption that "orbs" in photos are necessarily ghosts. But I agree that death isn't real, *not even for the body*. But there is a critical difference between Helder's beliefs about death and mine.

Helder, and most New Agers I know, look inward for answers. Their whole spirituality, and their relationships with others and the world, is based first and foremost on their relationships with themselves. That's not surprising, as we're all children of the "me" generation, brought up on advertising that exalts and caters to the self — and fills our minds with promises, promises, promises.

As one commentator put it: "The paranormal cannot be said to have caused Helder's bombing attacks, just as belief in UFOs did not directly cause the mass suicide of the Heaven's Gate cult in March of 1997.... Magical thinking in one part of a person's life can easily lead to a lack of critical thinking in others...."

I believe that basing a spirituality on "me" isn't only absurd, it's deadly. It leads not only to a lack of critical thinking, but to confusion and delusion.

As we'll see in the last chapter, we must look outward, not inward. If I've learned anything from long experience watching the multiverse work, it's that each person does *not* make his or her own reality. *All of us together make our common reality by drawing together the worlds to which we're most psychically connected.*

Given where many people's minds are these days, God help us.

The renowned British statesman Sir Edmund Burke (1729-1797) said words to the effect that people get the government they deserve. I could paraphrase that by stating hands-down that people get the *reality* they deserve.

As we saw in our down with individualism, up with personalism discussion in Chapter 4, our sense of self is an illusion that can shipwreck us if we try to base a spirituality or even a worldview on it. The sense of self exists only as a self-reference, a way to distinguish our own uniqueness from the unique people around us, whose lives and energies we intimately share as part of the Unity. That's personalism: Being unique and being part of the whole.

By contrast, the self as the individualist perceives it stands separate, sovereign and proud. It thinks that it is it, and that its body is it, too. It ends up alone, enslaved and frustrated.

Physicist, philosopher and self-described "quantum activist" Amit Goswami states here what I believe is the key to human existence. Better read this a few times. It takes some getting used to.

"Realize that the self of our self-reference is due to a tangled hierarchy, but our consciousness is the consciousness of the Being that is beyond the subject-object split. There is no other source of consciousness in the universe. The self of self reference and the consciousness of the original consciousness, make what we call self-consciousness."

The self doesn't exist any more than death does, and I believe that not admitting that has severe consequences. If there is an equivalent to death, it happens while we're alive. It's a death of the spirit and of the mind, and the best way to get to it is by concentrating on the self.

Is There Really No Death?

Death. The absence of life. Of all the mysteries that loom behind the question of God, ghosts and human destiny, death seems to be the ultimate one for all of us because we all fear what we don't know and don't understand. We are terrified of uncertainty.

I claim there is no such thing as death, but how can I do that? We watch our loved ones pass away, sometimes with terrible suffering. We bury friends, neighbors and strangers. We open the newspaper, and turn on the television, to news of random and wanton acts of violence and destruction. Deadly accidents, fires, disease, famine and suicides are everyday events. Wars and natural disasters rock the globe, usually affecting the poorest and weakest of us.

Death not only seems to exist, it seems to rule the world.

'And a Little Child Shall Lead Them....'

Not all my paranormal investigations consist of battles with nasty parasites, encounters with phantom oxcart drivers, or trying to find out who or what is tramping through someone's attic at 3 a.m. Once in awhile I get a case that's downright instructional, beautiful, even holy, and it usually involves guardians, especially ancestors.

In the spring of 1991, I was called in by a Connecticut family not because they were frightened, but because they wanted to share something marvelous that was happening in their home. Peter, their little boy of five, had been diagnosed with childhood leukemia, and he was getting a great deal of support from someone he had never known before.

"Peter suddenly started having long talks with my father, who died ten years before he was born!" the boy's mother told me. "When we ask Peter about it, he gets excited, not embarrassed." She said the boy told her "happy things" about her early life that only her father would have known.

From the first of my several visits, Peter took to me. Whenever I was there, he wouldn't leave my side, and we would go for walks hand in hand. This child was one of those special people whom it's a privilege to know: One who is "great souled."

Even though he was going through chemotherapy by this time, he was one of the happiest children I've ever met. His small body, which quickly deteriorated with the disease, contained the spirit of an angel, a lion, a god. As with nearly all children with terminal illnesses, Peter was other-centered. He wasn't the selfish little ego machine we so often associate with children. As with so many who face bodily death, Peter saw things as they really are, without ego, without excuse, realizing his precious Unity with all things.

Peter had conquered the paradox. He had attained peace within himself by forgetting himself. And there was nothing syrupy, sentimental or maudlin about it.

Peter saw the big picture with crystal clarity. He was so happy, he said, because his family, especially his grandpa, loved him so much and had told him so many "happy stories." One of these stories was about how big the world looks when you're little, but how little it looks when you're big.

"Grandpa says he's younger now, and he likes to climb trees because high up you can see more about the world," Peter chimed. "You can be a lot of different people. You can be anybody you want to be as long as you're together."

Asked in so many words if he was afraid of dying, Peter would drop a blockbuster like: "I won't die. My body's not me."

Peter's body passed in the bosom of his family in 1992. That very day, his great soul blossomed into a mighty guardian for them, and as long as I was in touch with the family I heard stories of Peter's constant love, guidance and protection for his loved ones. Peter even manifested himself in my life. He truly had "climbed higher" and "seen farther."

Peter's simple message brought home to me what life in the multiverse, and the stunning implications of the Unity, really mean for us.

I was reminded of *Isaiah* 11:1-10: "...a little child shall lead them."

Peter and his grandpa were right: From a higher, or even just a different, vantage point, we can see that what's around us in the world is a great deal less than what's really there. If we try, we really can see the big picture. We really can see that, in the multiverse, death not only is an illusion, its apparent power over us is the greatest illusion of all.

The reason is simple, once you start to get your mind around it.

Remember fractals? Picture a string of holiday lights as a fractal of the biosphere, with each of us as a light bulb. There are many bulbs, some of different colors and even different shapes, sizes and brightness. Sometimes a bulb is broken, or simply goes out and is discarded. Sometimes one is moved from one socket to another. All we see is the one string of lights and the building or Christmas tree it might be attached to.

We probably don't think of the big picture: This string we see is only one of billions through which the same unceasing power flows – around the corner or around the planet. Bulbs may come and go, but their power is part of the greater power, and it's never diminished.

This is a fractal of life in the multiverse.

Your conscious life is here and now as you read this book – on the "string of lights" you can see only from where you are, so to speak. I'm convinced that your subconscious, on the other hand, is your quite literal connection – your identity — with the billions of other "bulbs" that share the same source of power. They are not only your own other lives elsewhere and elsewhen in the multiverse – they are *all* lives.

Death is impossible in the multiverse not only because we ourselves — our bodies, our electromagnetism, our souls, our minds, our karma, or whatever other puny words we can contrive to describe the indescribable – are alive across many worlds at once.

Death is impossible because you are, at this instant, in one world or another; literally and absolutely; body, mind and all; still living the happiest moment of your life, though in your conscious life it's only what we call a memory. You're also still alive in your saddest and most terrible moment too. I believe that's what gives our conscious life balance, poignancy and spice.

The Unity is indiscriminate. In one world or another, you also are me. You share my memories and I share yours. And once you get a grip on this initially tough concept, it will hit you like a slap in the face. You'll know it's true.

Why don't we have a more conscious concept of these billions of shared lives? The background noise would be too much for us. Our species isn't yet to the point in its evolution where we could handle it. Depending on the society they live in, people who are consciously connected with other lives seem to be considered either holy or crazy. I'm absolutely convinced that what some religions call enlightenment and others call holiness is simply being conscious of lives the rest of us aren't conscious of. For those who understand it, *and can control it*, it's saintliness. For others, like those psychiatric patients I spoke about in Chapter 2, it's insanity.

It all depends on how you look at it and what you do with it. This puts sayings like, "That's what life is all about," in a whole new dimension – many new dimensions!

Even if we're "normal," we know this Unity is there, and we have frequent experiences of it. These can include things that have happened to all of us: Feeling an unexplainable bond with someone who's otherwise a stranger, feeling that "we were siblings from the start," or that "it was like we've known each other all our lives." Sometimes there's even the feeling that you *are* or *should be* someone else or someplace else.

I witnessed a beautiful example of shared lives after speaking at Mt. Ida College, just outside Boston, in 2004. I love speaking at colleges. I get intelligent, articulate questions from the students, and they love to share their own stories of paranormal experiences. At the end of my program the organizers usually plop me in an armchair somewhere, and the students line up to talk to me as though I were Santa Claus.

At Mt. Ida, two freshman girls came up and, intrigued by my ideas on human relationships within the multiverse, asked about their own.

"The first time we saw each other on the first day of the school year, we were drawn to each other, and we've been like sisters ever since. Why is that?" one asked.

"Because somewhere across the multiverse, in one world or another, you *are* each other," I replied. "We all share each other's lives, hopes and dreams subconsciously, but you two connected in such a way that it's conscious!"

I needed to say no more. Their eyes lit up, and they immediately grasped the whole idea.

"That explains it!" they both cried.

All for One, One for All

Death is impossible not only because in these worlds it's all *us*: one person in many bodies. All of us together – the entire biosphere - are one being in the Unity.

Once again, our race memory knows.

Ubuntu is an ancient Zulu word that forms the basis of the traditional African view of humanity and the world. It can simply mean "humanity," or it can mean "I am what I am because of who we all are." Its principle is: Everything I do affects you, everything you do affects me, everything we do affects the worlds.

It means that we are one. This is the Gaia Fact.

The most mistranslated and misinterpreted passage in the Christian New Testament, at least in the West, has to be *Matthew* 22:39. "Love your neighbor as yourself," which most of us interpret as "love your neighbor the way you love yourself." But in the original Greek (transliterated into the Roman alphabet), it says *agapesis ton plaision sou os seauton*: Love your neighbor *because he is* yourself.

There are other memories of our deathless nature reflected in myth and folklore.

The very ancient and widespread belief in reincarnation certainly fills the bill here. Having your body die, but your soul, spirit or essence live on to be reborn in another body is what you get when you know that death is fake, but you no longer understand quantum physics. Reincarnation in that sense is impossible simply because time in the multiverse doesn't have any more objective existence than death or the self do. Everything and everywhen exist at once. What we experience as past and future are simply functions of our consciousness. And if there's no past, there can't be past lives.

As we've seen, there are *simultaneous* lives, where we're already "reincarnated" many times over.

Some practical evidence for this is recounted in *Footsteps in the Attic: More First-Hand Accounts of the Paranormal in New England*, when I encounter some puzzled regression therapists whose subjects were talking about what appeared to be future lives or lives in alien worlds.

Belief in reincarnation almost certainly comes from the fact that we retain "memories" of other lives, which naturally are assumed to be from past lives. Moving from one body to another is not only a staple of eastern religions like Buddhism, Jainism and Hinduism, it turns up with surprising frequency in Judaism, where it's common in the esoteric tradition of the Kabbalah. It's not a mainstream Jewish doctrine, but it does come up in scholarly discussions. There's some evidence that the Essenes, members of one or more mysterious Jewish communities that existed about the time of Jesus, believed in reincarnation. There's even speculation that Jesus was an Essene.

Before St. Paul's version of Christianity triumphed over all others in the early centuries of the first millennium, there were reincarnation beliefs among several Christian sects, notably the Gnostics and others who had carried over beliefs common among the Greek pagans.

The much-venerated teacher of the Jain faith, Shrimad Rajchandra (1867-1908), wrote:

"The thoughtful person is neither happy nor unhappy about leaving this body behind. For him, the only death is turning away from the awareness of consciousness of soul or Atman. Not to be peaceful within oneself ... is the greatest loss and death itself. To be one with your own nature, to rest into knowledge only and to remain with your innermost self or soul, or the strongest desire for such a state of being removes even the fear of death."

Just like our worldly mother, the Jains believe, death gives us birth or rebirth.

"She is the savior. She changes the life of the evil and good. She transforms the pain and unhappiness and brings limitless bliss. She is the giver of liberation. She liberates us from the cycle of birth and rebirth."

That last statement indicates a big difference in the western and eastern approaches to this subject. Today belief in reincarnation is *de rigueur* for the western world's New Agers. Because I work with the paranormal, people assume that I also must levitate while meditating on past lives in my incense-filled study. I often get funny looks from these folks when I tell them that I don't believe in reincarnation – at least not in any classical sense of the term.

For the most part, eastern faiths consider reincarnation a pain in the neck, and they seek to break out of its cycle by attaining enlightenment. That's especially true when you have the prospect of reincarnating as, or "transmigrating" to, a cow, a frog or a gnat.

By contrast, many a western New Ager, disillusioned with organized religion and its stuffy salvation doctrines, generally heaves a hearty sigh of relief over the prospect of reincarnation. It means that his or her precious self isn't going to go "poof" upon bodily death. There's even a tendency to believe that we keep getting better from life to life as a matter of course.

Whether reincarnation is good or bad, "great souled" or "old souled" people like little Peter often are chalked up to it. They have such maturity and wisdom, it's said, because they have lived so many lives for so long a period of history. I've even heard a theory that modern society is generally "dumbing down" because of the planet's population explosion: There are too many "new souls" who haven't been around the block yet!

My approach is somewhat different, of course. Peter and those like him are "great souled" because they are in touch with the wisdom and goodness they have in lives they are already living elsewhere and elsewhen in the multiverse. They give new meaning to the pop terms "getting it together" and "living large"! It's as though they get 200 cable channels and the rest of us only get five. They're at home and in touch, and they can see farther because they have, in a manner of speaking, more eyes in more places at more times.

The Death of Death

Even in religions that don't officially recognize reincarnation or anything equivalent to it, there is the memory that death is an empty shell. For Christians, Jesus Christ destroyed death for every believer by descending into it at the Crucifixion:

"Death is swallowed up; victory is won! Oh death, where is thy victory? Oh death, where is thy sting?" (*1 Corinthians* 15:54-55)

The Orthodox Christian Easter service even has lines like: "Christ is risen, and not one dead remains in the grave!"

Others believe that death is non-existent, or at least defeatable, because they seek out contact with the "souls of the departed," and they get answers. Mediums, by whatever name, are as old as humanity, though today they are quite a bit more expensive.

Many mediums I know have great abilities when it comes to picking information out of other parts of the multiverse. The drawback is that I can count on the fingers of one hand the mediums who realize that's actually what they're doing. The rest are married to the sappy, two-dimensional, 19th century séance-room interpretation of what's happening. As a result, they see only what they want to see – or what their clients want them to see. In the end I don't think many of them have much of a clue.

Even worse, few mediums see the dark side of the multiverse, where our enemies lurk. To listen to most mediums, all you have to do is die, and you become some sort of super being standing constant vigilance over your family. Everything is always warm and fuzzy on "the other side," where the dear departed can nosh 'til they slosh without getting fat, play all the golf they want without greens fees, and watch television all day without a brain drain.

What really scares me about mediums is that they seem to assume that every "message" they receive not only is true but comes from whomever it says it comes from. Between most mediums and the hideously dangerous practices of Ouija boards and séances, it's a parasite playground.

What's really ironic to me about my own opinion of mediums is that, given the nature of life and lives in the multiverse, it's a near certainty that everyone we consider "dead" here *really is* chowing down chocolates, sipping a beer or socking a soccer ball somewhere elsewhere or elsewhen!

And that's why I said at the beginning that this chapter is so dangerous.

If we, something like Luke Helder, think that deliberately hopping worlds through bodily death is an "easy out," a one-way ticket away from our problems, even a quick way to somehow help others, we're in for, quite literally, a very rude awakening.

What Happens When we Die?

So we come to the Big One: What really happens to you when your body dies? Whatever happens, it isn't death. Our lives *cannot* end. As little Peter said, our bodies aren't us.

Our life – conscious and subconscious — reaches out in vast waves across the multiverse, across the biosphere, mind to mind, body to body, soul to soul, hand to hand, age to age, world to world. The departure of the consciousness from a body that has been used up – is no more serious than a flake of skin falling off your finger – or a bulb breaking on our string of proverbial Christmas lights. The energy already fills another bulb, sharing its life with all.

"Where you go" is up to you. I believe that we truly "make our own bed" in the multiverse, so the "you" your conscious mind switches to after you use up where you are now probably takes the path of least resistance, like everything else in Nature.

If you're a selfish jerk with no clue about the Unity, you'll continue to be a selfish jerk, and this is the kind of thing the eastern religions dread. No growth, stagnation, certainly is a kind of spiritual death. If you're a predator who lives off the weak and takes joy in the suffering of others, someone so ferociously egocentric that the Unity would spit you out if it could, there are backward steps in the multiverse, too. Worlds of endless aloneness, even terror for the terrible: Call it hell and you won't be wrong.

It's not impossible at all that these people might switch to the consciousness of a parasite. As I said, the Unity is indiscriminate.

If, on the other hand, you've realized that you are nothing without the rest of us, or at least without your loved ones, your consciousness probably will shift to a world where *you're already* a benevolent ancestor or a guide for others – perhaps a human angel – body and all. Bodily death means nothing but a shift from one body to another...very much like changing the channel on your television set or changing a bulb on our string of lights.

Taking this idea to the max, you also might switch to the consciousness of a benign but, to us, completely alien world and life form, and on with life you go.

While their beliefs are couched in myth, reincarnation adherents from eastern traditions probably have it about right. If you don't move closer to the Unity (enlightenment) in your conscious life, you won't draw close to it in your closest subconscious lives. So when your subconscious becomes consciousness in another body, your life is likely to be another dead-end existence. If, however, you grow closer to the Unity in your conscious life, you will draw to yourself those subconscious lives, those "bubble worlds," in which you are more enlightened, and that will be your destination.

Each of us is going through bodily death at one or another place in the multiverse at every moment. That car you nearly stepped in front of, you *did* step in front of somewhere or somewhen else. In a thousand other corners of the multiverse, that benign growth you just had surgically removed was a deadly cancer.

The transition of bodily death is probably the root experience of our entire existence. But this experience is only the first clue to our ultimate destiny, and we'll deal with the rest in our final two chapters.

Why the Death Experience at All?

In the meantime, the question arises: Why do we have to go through bodily death at all, especially when there's loss and suffering involved? What's the point of these frequent shifts of consciousness from one world to another?

For the same reason that popular concepts of heaven eventually would turn out to be hell: Boredom. We're just not built for it.

Like our whole biosphere, we are creatures created not only to create but to change. Nothing is more deadly to us than sameness. Our minds grow dull. Excitement dies within us. We have nothing to look forward to. No matter how rich we may be, no matter how many big-screen TVs or six-packs we use to distract ourselves, boredom is a death sentence for human beings. We need change and, hopefully, growth. The experience of bodily death is the signature and root of that change.

Bodily death is our ticket to survival.

9

Finding God

*Love is the magician, the enchanter, that changes worthless
things to joy, and makes right royal kings and queens of
common clay. It is the perfume of that wondrous flower, the
heart, and without that sacred passion, that divine swoon,
we are less than beasts; but with it,
earth is heaven, and we are gods.*
- Robert Green Ingersoll
American Lawyer, Author, Agnostic

We moderns are among the few people in human history who
are lost enough, disunited enough, selfish enough and, I might
even say, dense enough to even ask the question: Is there really
a God?

There has been the occasional voice of unbelief here and there
throughout history. That's been true even, as we have seen, in a
few significant religions. But among the overwhelming masses
of people in every age, both educated and uneducated, asking if
there is a God would have been like asking if there is air or grass
or animals.

Such a question can be conceived only from ignorance of the Unity.

But wait! We must be fair to our poor species. We've seen so much misunderstanding, complication, bloodshed, betrayal, and just plain confusion over God and gods in the course of this book, I think we're quite justified in asking what and where He, She or It really is.

I think we have to start by using what writers and teachers sometimes employ to describe the indescribable or express the inexpressible. There's even a term for it in theology – the "apophatic" approach: describing God by what He, She or It is *not*.

Say the Word!

First off, we've been using this "He, She or It" stuff long enough! In this case, the problem isn't God or even us. It's our language. No human language I know of, let alone a modern one like English, is quite up to actually talking about God. We can't even decide what to call God. The word "god" itself is a common noun that can be applied to any deity.

We have such trouble talking about God because language is a tool to convey knowledge, and we can't know God by knowledge. We know God by experience, and the best we can do to describe God is by using analogies: God is like this. God does this. God isn't like that. Mix this problem with today's insecure, even paranoid, attitudes, especially a terror of political incorrectness, and we're up the creek to the point of comedy.

A certain American Christian denomination drew guffaws from around the planet when its 2006 general assembly got bogged down in trying to make God politically correct. Believing that the traditional Holy Trinity was "sexist," well intentioned delegates tied themselves into knots coming up with terms like "Mother, Child and Womb."

At the time I was a little flummoxed as to why "Father" would be sexist and "Mother" wouldn't.

Then there was the proposed "Rock, Redeemer and Friend." Huh?

No end of amused, Rod Dreher, editor of the Sunday commentary section of *The Dallas Morning News*, staged a "Name That Trinity" contest. Among the suggestions were "Class Act, Cuddler and Confidante," "Rock, Scissors and Paper" and "Larry, Curly and Moe."

The Father, Son and Holy Spirit, by the way, survived the election.

As we saw earlier, the ancient Hebrews were so aware of language's inadequacies that they didn't even use God's name. They used words that amounted to "You-Know-Who." The farthest they went linguistically was something like "Lord."

We can safely agree that our Primal God cannot be known through human language, but we move along nonetheless. In English, "he" technically is gender-neutral when referring to God or humanity as a whole. So let's just stick with good old He for now.

So much for language.

Religion, Right or Wrong?

Can we know God through religion?

That may seem like a funny question, since most of us have been taught that religion is precisely where God is supposed to be found. By implication it's also where He's supposed to stay so that He doesn't disturb our daily lives, or make us feel uncomfortable about the way we live or how we treat others. But it's a loaded question if ever there was one.

Actually, religion is supposed to be the bag of tools we use to get to God, both as individuals and as a group. God-centered religions all claim to have books, practices, messiahs, gurus, saints, bishops, and what-have-you, that provide what they always claim is the "right" way to God. But religion also has been a large part of the problem in human history.

While pagan religions not based on parasite-worship tended to be more tolerant than the latter-day "people of the book," all religions seem to have involved too high a comfort level at one time or another. By that I mean that they became too settled, too pleased with themselves, too institutionalized – too comfortable. Most evolved a clergy class, frequently all-male, some of whom often were – and are – concerned more with protecting the institution, and their own job security, than with the truth. The official doctrines within these religions sometimes have mauled the image of God in terrible ways: creating a vengeful demon God meant more to keep people from thinking and straying than to bring them to full and honest Unity. Religion and its institutions have too often taken on lives of their own and become ends in themselves.

In spirituality always beware of being too comfortable!

I know as deeply as anyone that religion, in one of its many forms, can and does work for huge numbers of people. The various teachings, worship, spiritual experiences, and techniques for prayer and meditation can touch the souls of millions in ways nothing else can. Something in us responds to the religious. But I still don't think that any one religion is enough to restore the Unity in which I believe our Primal God is to be recovered.

If anything, organized religion sometimes has furthered the multiversal division. Worse, too many people don't seek God through religion, they *equate* God with religion. And this has had horrific results for some very good people who probably ought to have known better.

I'm thinking especially of the most frustrated person I ever met. He was an avowed atheist who had a spiritual temperament. His entire experience of God, such as it was, came through religion, and he never could bring himself to separate any notion of a Supreme Being from the "blatant nonsense" he had been taught about God as a child by his strictly Orthodox, synagogue-going parents.

My friend, and so many others like him, also reject God because they are kind hearted. That's right. Because they can't separate God from religion, they reject God if they see hypocrisy, injustice, cruelty or bloodshed condoned or even carried out by members of a given religion or their leaders.

I've always thought that Robert G. Ingersoll (1833-1899), a leading agnostic writer of the 19th century, is a perfect example of this. As quoted by his friend and biographer, I. Newton Baker, Ingersoll was irate with the biblical God, and the religions that preached Him, for being so nasty:

"While the Old Testament threatens men, women and children with disease, famine, war, pestilence and death, there are no threatenings of punishment beyond this life. The doctrine of eternal punishment is a dogma of the New Testament. This doctrine, the most cruel, the most infamous, is taught, if taught at all, in the Bible — in the New Testament. One cannot imagine what the human heart has suffered by reason of the frightful doctrine of eternal damnation. It is a doctrine so abhorrent to every drop of my blood, so infinitely cruel, that it is impossible for me to respect either the head or heart of any human being who teaches or fears it. This doctrine necessarily subverts all ideas of justice. To inflict infinite punishment for finite crimes, or rather for crimes committed by finite beings, is a proposition so monstrous that I am astonished it ever found lodgment in the brain of man. Whoever says that we can be happy in heaven while those we loved on earth are suffering infinite torments in eternal fire, defames and calumniates the human heart."

Like the rest of us, Ingersoll longed for God. I will never

believe otherwise of him. But because the only God he ever knew came to him through religion, he never found a God worthy of his love.

Ingersoll writes about Christmas:

"Again we celebrate the victory of Light over Darkness, of the God of day over the hosts of night.... In the embrace of Isis, Osiris rises from the dead, and the scowling Typhon is defeated once more. Again Apollo, with unerring aim, with his arrow from the quiver of light, destroys the serpent of shadow.... Again Buddha by a miracle escapes from the tyrant of Madura, Zoroaster foils the King, Bacchus laughs at the rage of Cadmus, and Chrishna eludes the tyrant....

"This is the festival of the sun-god, and as such let its observance be universal. This is the great day of the first religion, the mother of all religions — the worship of the sun. Sun worship is not only the first, but the most natural and most reasonable of all. And not only the most natural and the most reasonable, but by far the most poetic, the most beautiful.... The sun is the all-seeing, the all-pitying, the all-loving. This bright God knew no hatred, no malice, never sought for revenge."

Ingersoll may or may not have been aware that the Christian Church deliberately adopted pagan sun-feast days as Christian holidays, including Christmas, in its competition with the Roman religion of *Sol Invictus* (the Invincible Sun). The Hebrew Prophet Malachi refers to the rising of the "Sun of Righteousness" (*Malachi* 4:2), which Christians interpret as a prophecy of Jesus Christ.

In any case, one visitor described the atmosphere in Ingersoll's home as, among other positive things, "holy." There are many stories of Ingersoll's kind heart. I think that had he actually opened himself up to looking for God outside the realm of fierce doctrines and men in starched collars, he might have become a spiritual giant. Maybe, down deep, he did and he was.

To atheists and agnostics, however, Ingersoll is a hero. He should be a hero also to all who seek for God. Ingersoll spent a lifetime demonstrating, but I don't think ever believing, that God and religion are *not* the same thing.

God as Cosmic Teddy Bear

Similarly, plenty of people reject God – or what they think is God — because of all the suffering they see in the world, whether abetted by religions or not. The warm, fuzzy, comfortable, middle-class God often projected by religions naturally seems to be a lie when you watch the evening news. It also seems to be a lie when you yourself are poor amidst plenty, hungry, abused, unemployed, sick or despondent with failure or loss, and especially if you witness the suffering of your own children.

It's easy to have faith on a full stomach and an ample wallet.

If there is a God, many feel, He must be cruel and uncaring. Often enough, it gets personal. How many people "lose their faith," "stop going to church" or "stop praying" when a loved one passes? How many children are poisoned against the very idea of God when they're told asinine things like, "God took mommy to be with Him in heaven"? How many others turn against God if they don't "have their prayers answered" in the form of the money for that snazzy car, the job or promotion they want, or if their grandiose life plans don't materialize.

We get mad at God because He doesn't come barreling in and fix everything. "If He's all-powerful, why doesn't He…." But what God ever told us that we're somehow entitled to be healthy, wealthy and wise, and that it's His job to wait on us until we are? God isn't the government. Who says He owes us anything? Because too many religions have implied that God is that "great vending machine in the sky," He is by far humanity's favorite scapegoat because we're our own favorite spoiled children.

Our Missing Mother

There's another fatal problem with many organized modern religions, especially the Big Three. They have robbed us of our Mother.

From what we can see of our most ancient legends, traditions and even documents, one aspect that was very present and very balanced in our Primal God was the presence of the Divine Female. She was the wife of Huve, Paluga or Baiame in our Primal Godhead. But She lived on in the mysterious Shekinah of *Genesis* times; the beautiful Isis, beloved of Egypt and the whole Mediterranean region in more recent times; and in many more whose names we may or may not know, before and since. As our species aged and the Unity faded, She became an anchor for those of us who remembered.

It's theologically damnable to say so, but She lives on among the Eastern Orthodox and the Roman Catholics in the gentle love of the Blessed Virgin Mary, the mother of Jesus; in doctrine the "Theotokos, she who gave birth to God." In the teaching of these ferociously male-dominated churches, Mary is most emphatically *not* a goddess. But anyone with a lick of historical and theological sense can see that She is, and She's there for one reason: The common people absolutely refused – and refuse today – to relinquish our Mother. A special saint with unique abilities to intercede with her Son, Jesus, Mary is divine in all but name.

In the Chinese philosophy-religion of Taoism, our Mother was remembered as the female principle of life and the Earth – the Yin – who opposes yet balances the male principle – the Yang – in all things.

She lives on in other ways too. Devotion to Isis, first honored in ancient Egypt as an agricultural Goddess and the All-Mother, is more widespread and devout now than it has been since ancient times, a New Age phenomenon that I believe is taking root with many who might be considered otherwise outside the New Age movement.

Devotion to other goddesses is springing up, too, among men as well as women.

The power of the Divine Feminine, and Her ability to touch the human soul, cannot be underestimated. Whether called Isis, Hathor, Athena, Diana, Brigit, Panu, Pele or a thousand others, She's back. Even if the name used is based on a vague memory of one of the more beneficent intruders, perhaps Ninlil or Ninkharsag, our staunch race-memory of the Original undoubtedly lies behind it.

You *can* approach God in religion, and your faith and spirituality *can* prosper in that context! But even with a return to the Divine Feminine, can we find the Unity to make religion complete again? Maybe, but just remember that being religious and being Godly are two different things.

Nevertheless, we may be getting closer.

Is God Green or Gray?

Could God really have been an alien?

Many who believe the Paleocontact Theory suspect that the intruders we met in Chapter 6 were here so early in human prehistory that they're responsible for our whole concept of the divine. Before that, they contend, there was no "Primal God," no clear idea of a Supreme Being. Perhaps, as Ingersoll implied, the earliest people simply worshipped the sun, and every religion and every god or goddess descends from that first faith experience.

Is God really based on our earliest encounters with parasites and intruders, or perhaps even ancestors and guardians?

I don't believe that for a minute.

Remember the Dream Time, the Time before Time? Its story told for at least 65,000 years, it's the earliest remembered tradition among the oldest tribes that still exist. I believe these race memories tell not only of a different God than we meet later, but of a different – a United – world that existed long before Ehden/Eden, Yahweh and the terrible "Wars of the Gods." There is an entirely different "feel" to the world of the primeval All-Father Baiame than there is to that of the Most High Anu. I believe the former existed many millennia before the latter ever happened.

While there are many gods and spirits in the Dream Time, some good and some bad (guardians and parasites, just like today), there is that clear Supreme Being. There is the Sky God and his very Trinity-like family. Unlike the situation we see in the later *Atra-Hasis* or *Kharsag Epics*, humans come across as beloved children of God, not slaves, klutzes or pawns.

For the Australian Aborigines especially, the Dream Time was nice and simple. The Lord God Baiame created the world and enjoyed its beauty just as they did, and He appointed man and woman together to take care of the Earth, which was itself a living thing.

Interestingly, Baiame also told them to be vegetarians!

The Dream Time's Creation story is in line with the order science accepts, albeit in the guise of folklore. Instead of a colony of *Elohim* building irrigation canals, raising crops and genetically manipulating humans, we find the All-Father taking the sun for His wife and giving birth to the Earth and celestial bodies. It's believed, of course, that Earth and the rest of the solar planets actually were "born" from the sun as the whole system split into solid bodies and cooled.

As the Dream Time story continues, the Sun Mother opens her eyes, and darkness flees from the Earth. The planet's atmosphere is born from her breath, and She crosses the land from east to west, causing plants to spring up. With their potential already in the Earth, She awakens the other living creatures, and they themselves become creators.

So was our Primal God an alien? In the eyes of later peoples, His successors may have been, but I'm convinced that the Original isn't.

In their need to explain the unexplainable, our distant ancestors certainly used symbols like the Sun, Moon and natural phenomena to help make God more understandable. When the parasites realized what they'd been missing, and made us think they were gods, we got confused enough. When the intruders stopped by and realized they could get a good thing going with us as pawns, they adopted – or we applied to them — the more ancient and obvious God symbols.

With our natural desire for God burning within us, it was the best we could do.

Is God Just Us?

Many people, especially atheists, suspect that most or all human experiences of God are the products of misunderstood phenomena within us. Temporal-lobe action in the brain, interaction between our own bioelectric fields and other electromagnetic phenomena are possible candidates.

While I certainly ran into cases of "voices" inside people's heads while a graduate student in psychology, I've never seen any psycho-physical explanation come close to the reality of either paranormal or God experiences. That's especially true when these experiences are shared by more than one person and/or include independent phenomena.

As comforting as atheists might find the "it's all in your head" theory, that just doesn't cut it.

We are not God. We are the Child and the hand of God.

Is God All-Natural?

Is God the same as Nature?

There is a belief called "pantheism," that everything that exists forms God and that God consists of everything that exists. Many pantheists would especially identify God with Nature.

Any pantheist worth his or her salt would immediately pick up on my use and concept of the word Unity in this book, recognizing the whole process of finding God in the Unity and finding the Unity in God.

Pantheism has many definitions and many forms, but they are all variations on the theme that everything equals God and God equals everything. Pantheism or tendencies toward it are present in spiritualities, religions and philosophies as far back as we'd care to look. As a rule, the closer a culture was to the Earth, the more pantheistic its outlook tended to be. Conversely, the further a culture drifted from its hunter-gatherer or agricultural roots, and the closer it got to artificial environments and machine rule, pantheism would turn up again, like some sort of reaction to an unnatural way of life.

Pantheism is a common spiritual tendency in our post-industrial society today.

Among the ancient philosophers, theologians and writers whose influence is with us today, elements of pantheism can be found in Plato of Greece (c. 427-c. 347 B.C.), Plotinus of Egypt and Rome (205-270 B.C.), and Lao Tze of China (6th century B.C.). More modern names include the philosophers Baruch Spinoza (1632-1677) and Georg Hegel (1770-1831), the astronomer and Roman Catholic priest Giordano Bruno (1548-1600), the Christian theologians John Scotus Eriugena (815-877) and Paul Tillich (1886-1965), and even the great scientist Albert Einstein (1879-1955).

The Indian scripture the *Bhagavad Gita* has many pantheistic elements.

Because of exposure to the ancient Greek philosophers, especially Plato, many of whose manuscripts they preserved, some

Muslim philosophers and mystics of the Middle Ages adopted pantheistic ideas. There was a merging of Western and Eastern pantheistic thought in some areas of Muhammedanism, and several European thinkers since then, such as Rene Guenon (1886-1951), were so impressed with this that they became Muslims.

Literally hundreds of eminent poets, writers, artists and composers from around the globe in all periods had pantheistic phases or elements in their works. You can include some not-so-eminent writers too, like Paul F. Eno.

Today pantheism, in one form or another, is very big among New Agers, who tend to have great respect for the planet. So is pantheism, at long last, our path back to the Unity and our Primal God?

It's probably the closest we've come yet but, alas, our answer is still incomplete. Close, but no cigar!

As we've learned bitterly amid the environmental crisis, humans are part of Nature, not separate from it. As we have traveled through this book together, perhaps you've picked up a picture of humanity as happier, better balanced and more unified when we were working with Nature instead of against it. Pantheism as a natural faith appeals to more people in more places than probably any other approach to God. But I think it has a big problem with size: In pantheism's strictest sense, God gets lost in its midst. At the same time, it's too small to contain God. God is more than just Nature, more than just us. He's more than just the multiverse.

Nature is no more God than our bodies are us. Nature is a mirror of God as our bodies are mirrors of us.

In Our Own Way

I, as with most of you, believe in a personal God, a Supreme Being Who cares for each and every being in the multiverse, just as we care for every finger, toe and limb of our own bodies.

I learned to love this God when I was a child. I walk with Him, I pray to Him, I live and work by His side, and Jackie and I taught our children to do the same.

He is my Father, She is my Mother, and we are Their child.

The problem with most of us is precisely that "I." In our last chapter, the one about death, we said that the only real way to die is to concentrate on the self. And it's the same problem with all the possible paths to God we've examined so far: They're too individualistic. They can only go so far because "I'm" at the center of the viewpoint, so the viewpoint is too narrow. We are in our own way, complete with all our doubting "baggage."

We're too weighed down with the self and with fears that we'll believe the wrong thing. We're too weighed down with baggage to climb high and see far, as our little friend Peter said we must.

As we've said, individualism doesn't work. In the multiverse, we express our uniqueness through the whole biosphere, and the whole biosphere expresses its uniqueness through us. As an individualist, you can compete with your brother-in-law over who has the biggest television, you can claw your way up the corporate ladder, and you can cut off that old lady at the intersection. You can live the life of an amoeba: pursuing food and avoiding pain. But you can't have a true picture, or be a true mirror, of anything that's real, let alone God.

Remember our quantum theology, as Sister Rita so simply expressed it?

"Quantum theology emphasizes the experience of the divine as told by the myriad of members making up the human experience, regardless of creed. It dismantles exclusivity so as to affirm that we are all connected."

Without the Unity we cannot fulfill our destiny – not even as individuals. Why, in so many religions, are angels considered extensions of God? *Because all life is shared, especially God's.*

We rediscover our Primal God by rediscovering each other. And in doing so, we find ourselves.

Destiny Calls

What, then, is human destiny?

It's a fractal of the family. It's to be the Child of the Father and the Mother. Just as our children grow up to be adults, we as Children are called to grow up to become what our Parents are. It's to take the next step in our evolution. *Our destiny is to be gods and goddesses ourselves.*

This is hinted at in New Age thinking, and it's even present in theology.

Many early pagans, especially the Greeks, used terms like "theosis," meaning deification, or actually becoming a god. The poet Callimachus (305-240 B.C.) used the term and believed in it. Among the neoplatonist philosophers, especially those devoted to the Goddess Athena, there were Iamblichus (250-330) and Proclus (412-486). Even Flavius Claudius Iulianus (331-363), the Roman emperor vilified by the Christians as "Julian the Apostate" for deciding to return to paganism, was a theosis believer.

As it did with many pagan ideas, the early Christian Church adopted theosis and Christianized it. People like St. Athanasius the Great (298-373) and St. Maximus the Confessor (589-682) talked about people becoming by grace what God is by nature, all made possible by God the Son becoming human as Jesus Christ. As Athanasius put it, "God became man that man might become God."

The primary contention of this book is that men and women *already are gods and goddesses together in the Unity*, and already share the life of our Primal God. We just have to accept it, believe it and use it.

Moving to Square Two

Square one is just as it was when this book began. It's divesting ourselves of the conviction that we really and truly *know* anything. It's doing the best we can with Aristotle's *tabula rasa*. It's doing the best we can with what we see and experience. It's doing everything that modern society tells us is lame, unnecessary and unprofitable.

It's starting our quest for God with utter simplicity, no preconceived notions, and with complete openness to whatever may happen. It's listening without speaking. It's learning to be silent. It's learning to be humble. It's learning to live together. It's learning to learn all over again. Worst of all, it's learning to stand naked before the Truth.

It's learning to do without quick spiritual "fixes," and to do hard spiritual work, maybe for years to come.

These are all things that terrify modern humans – especially silence.

Let's let God start us off by showing us simplicity, for He Himself is, above all, humble.

I Shall Be

The simplest self-description of God I have ever been able to find in any ancient text is from the Hebrew Bible. In *Exodus* 3:14, Moses, standing before the famous "burning bush," asks God His Name, and he gets: היהא רשא היהא   *"Ehyeh Asher Ehyeh."* "I Shall Be Who I Shall Be." In English, this usually ends up translated "I Am Who Am," which I think miserably misses the point.

I believe these three simple Hebrew words contain the answer to every question we've asked in this book. How can language begin to express it? Our Primal God is the Life, Soul and Pulse of everything and everyone, as the pantheists believe, but in Himself is far more.

God is the Future and Goal of the multiverse. As Teilhard de Chardin might say, He is what "He Shall Be": The "Omega Point," the Destination Who will draw all Creation back across the infinite worlds to the Unity. And as this stupendous cosmic drama unfolds, God holds the tiny hand of the tiniest child – as that child lives in joy, or as its conscious body passes in injustice, pain and horror -- caused not by God but by our wanton disUnity. And God holds its hand still as its new but ancient consciousness awakens elsewhere and elsewhen – deeper, wiser, holier and more alive than ever.

Language conveys knowledge, and the Unknowable cannot be known. God must be experienced. To do that, we must first lose everything.

Like any good parent with children who need to stand on their own two feet, God will hold our hands, but He isn't going to do it all for us. God has given us the tools to do it ourselves, and He expects us to use them.

We must *accept, believe* and *act.*

The multiverse is waiting.

10

Connecting the Dots

It takes two to tell the truth –
one to say it and one to hear it.
Henry David Thoreau, *American author*

This book began with the crazy idea that the paranormal isn't just spooks and monsters. It can point the way toward some pretty important stuff, like rediscovering God, finding our true nature, and fulfilling our destiny as a species. It's about learning to be alive all over again. We reach into the more enlightened lives we are already living elsewhere or elsewhen in the multi-verse, and draw them into our conscious lives here and now.

The real trick is learning to do it as a community.

Let's wrap it up.

• Our conscious world is one of a countless number of worlds spread out across a vast multiverse. Within these worlds is contained all realities and all possibilities. All pasts, all futures, all beings, all things that can possibly exist are contained within the multiverse. That includes all possible "us's."

• Like a plant with roots branching out far from its trunk, we exist in the multiverse in every possible form we can take. We have one spirit and live one life across the worlds in many different bodies and forms, but very few of us have reached the point in our evolution where we can be conscious of more than one body at a time. That's why the vast majority of our life is subconscious.

• We also share the lives of all other people, all other creatures, all other things in the biosphere throughout the multiverse. That's why we can't have a meaningful existence, never mind a successful spiritual life, if we concentrate just on our conscious selves. It's not about me. It's not about you. It's about us.

• What's a successful spiritual life? It starts by learning to be fully alive in the Unity that exists behind it all. It's there that we rediscover God – Him, Her and Us -- uncorrupted by petty and divisive ideas we got from paranormal "outside influences," either in human history or in our personal lives. It's also where we rediscover each other, and the precious uniqueness of each one.

A successfully spiritual person sees vividly just how crucial it is for us to take care of each other.

• Our destiny is to recover our own group power as the Divine Child, to become gods and goddesses as our Father and Mother are God. Then we can work with God to save our species, heal our planet, and take the next step in our evolution.

A Very Long Memory

Don't take it from me. Take it from a guy whose memory goes back about 30,000 years.

In the course of my military service I spent a grand total of seven hours in Australia. But it was time well spent. While waiting for transport out of a rural area near Melbourne that day, I got talking with, of all people, an aged, wrinkled, cheerful Aborigine named Mindiluwi. He was about four feet tall, and he couldn't have weighed more than ninety pounds.

By the time our conversation ended, though, I was convinced that Mindiluwi was a giant.

He told me all about God, ghosts and human destiny from the very long viewpoint of his people. He spoke of what I'd later call fractals, life paradoxes, self-fulfillment through self-forgetfulness, and starting at square one to build a spiritual life. And when I shared my own experiences of investigating the paranormal, and my budding theories about what it all might mean, Mindiluwi not only knew what I was talking about, he shed much light on it. I think I learned more in my few hours of talk with him than I did in years of reading books by every other luminary mentioned in this book.

The Aborigines talk about "guruwari," seeds of life planted in the Earth by their original ancestors during the Dream Time. These seeds are the spark of life in all things, including you and me. Not only that, but the guruwari contain *the dream of what can be again.* This matters, because for the Aborigines, dreams are very, very real. Everything is created and exists through dreams. That means the Dream Time is the most real thing of all.

Dreaming is the Aborigines' way of explaining what we've been saying. Our psychic power as a species reaches out into the multiverse and pulls in worlds where what we need to be real *is* real. The more people who dream – the more who realize the Unity and work together – the more real the dream becomes in our conscious world.

Accepting and welcoming the guruwari within you is where *you* must begin in helping to dream a new life for *all of us.*

Just as a seed, alone in the dark, damp Earth, contains all

kinds of possibilities, it's the same with us. A seed thirsts for water, and to be what it was meant to be; we thirst for God and for the Unity God created us to dream. Each of us is a fractal of that seed.

Okay, fine. So what do we do? Let's let the simple wisdom of Mindiluwi tell us.

Step One: Accept

"Your people are always confused and sorry for yourselves," Mindiluwi said, his tiny eyes shining in his warm face. "You have trouble believing that things are really simple, and that there really isn't anything to worry about."

We accept and welcome our guruwari by simply accepting the reality of the multiverse and everything we've said about it. That includes accepting God. If you think you're an atheist or agnostic, I know Mindiluwi would tell you to grow up and get over it.

Quit fighting, rationalizing, analyzing, and pretending that you know anything; that's his message. Just accept. In doing this, you're not "checking your mind at the door," you're taking it, and your whole self, to a higher level in order to, as little Peter would say, "see far."

In our daily activities and interactions, with all the negative energy they can produce, we use our minds only in "first gear." How far do you get when you drive a car only in first gear? By using a tool like meditation to take our mind into acceptance, then awareness, of the multiverse, we're using our mind as it was meant to be used – in all five gears!

Once you accept what reality really is, you can start clearing the noise and garbage out of your life so you can attune yourself *to your entire self* throughout the multiverse. Through this can come divine awareness, insight, deepening relationships with friends, loved ones (including those who have passed), and even those we so unknowingly call "strangers." Most of all, you will grow in the Unity.

But we're not gods in our conscious world yet! We have problems, fears, personal issues, interpersonal difficulties, addictions, quirks – all sorts of challenges. Meditating yourself into a state of acceptance will help cut even your worst problems down to size because you'll not only see what reality really is, but what your problems really are. You'll have a clearer mind and clearer answers. You'll realize that you can do it.

"Just be quiet and tell yourself you will accept the truth," Mindiluwi told me. "Just shut up and listen to the quiet."

Being quiet. How do you do that in the "wired" 21st century? I can't think of anything we're more afraid of, or that's harder to come by, than silence.

But, as Mindiluwi might say, "Deal with it."

All the noise in our lives makes it easy to hide. It makes it easy *not* to accept the guruwari. Quieting the heart and soul leads to honesty: seeing things the way they really are, and that makes us nervous. But it leads to acceptance, and accepting something, whether it be good or bad, is always "half the battle" toward achieving or conquering it.

Hard as it may be at first, we quiet the heart, and start attuning ourselves to the multiverse, through meditation.

• Realize from the start there's no slam-bang way to achieve this new, enlightened, powerful and divine life in the multiverse. Commit yourself to wanting it and working for it. It'll be worth it.

• If you have a life partner or close friends, this is a quest you can make together. If he, she or they aren't interested, explain yourself patiently, let it go, and do it on your own.

• If you already know basic meditation techniques, you're ahead of the game.

• You'll meditate better if you eat intelligently. Organic is always good. Eat a balanced diet, and try to avoid heavy foods. There's a good reason for that. People in the western world don't understand the concept of fasting as a religious practice, let alone a good health habit. The point of fasting is not to "sacrifice," "chasten yourself" or "give up" anything. It's to reduce bodily digestive functions so that the mind can concentrate on prayer, meditation and clear seeing in order to commune with God.

Healthwise, of course, keeping hormones, chemicals and other preservatives out of your system is always good.

• Find a place to be alone and silent for meditation. It must be a place where you won't be disturbed, and where you feel completely at ease. This will be your sanctuary. It can be an unused room in your house, a tool shed in your yard, a bench in a garden, a clearing in the woods, a chair in your bedroom, or even your car.

• Tough as your schedule may be, make time each day to spend alone and in silence. Twice a day, twenty minutes at a time, is ideal but not always possible.

• Turn off the music, the cell phone, the telephone and every other electronic device in the room, including the computer. Electropollution will hinder your efforts. Some people meditate to music, but that won't help here.

• It's the hardest part of this whole effort: You must practice and practice clearing your mind of all the useless, uncontrolled thoughts and impressions that flit through it all day long. Different techniques work for different people, but few can achieve silence simply by sitting there and trying to force their minds to be quiet. A "mantra," a word to meditate upon, works as a focus for many people. I suggest choosing a divine name that resonates in your own mind, heart and spirit: one that makes you feel warm, protected and comfortable.

It can be "Jesus," it can be "Isis," it can be "Huve," it can be a loved one, or just a word that works for you. It can be the name of a guardian. Often *a guardian will choose you* rather than the other way around. Sometimes it's an angel or an ancestor. Be open but be careful. If a guardian doesn't feel *absolutely right or comfortable* for you, it's probably not a guardian. Trust your instincts, not your wishful thinking.

"Remember that there are dangerous spirits too. Don't talk to any spirit that doesn't make you feel right," Mindiluwi warned.

This is the same advice I give to people during paranormal investigations. As humanity has learned to its cost, we have brilliant enemies as well as willing friends in the multiverse. If anything you encounter during meditation makes you uncomfortable, *detach immediately* and start over.

It's unlikely, but still possible, that a parasite may be attached to the area you've chosen for meditation, or may have its eye on you or your family for one reason or another. This will make you feel uncomfortable, and you should deal with it by using the techniques I suggest in Appendix III of the first edition of *Footsteps in the Attic: More First-Hand Accounts of the Paranormal in New England* (2002). As of this writing, the same material is available online at http://www.newenglandghosts.com/what_to_do.htm.

• Meditate according to whatever technique works best for you, as long as it's in silence. If you're a beginner, I suggest sitting in a comfortable but armless chair, your hands and arms resting, fingers open, on your legs. Don't cross your legs, arms or fingers, as this will crimp energy and blood flow.

• Breathing in through your mouth and out through your nose, calm yourself by *visualizing* all your negative energy (stresses, pains, fears, hates and doubts) flowing slowly from the top of your head, down through your shoulders, down your arms and out through your fingertips, like smoke. Do the same with your lower body, letting the negative energy flow down your trunk, down your legs and out through your toes.

Then breathe normally.

• Use all your attention and all your energy to focus on your mantra, repeating it again and again *in time with your breathing*. Use this technique, or whatever variation of it works best for you, until you no longer need to use your mantra, and can meditate silently, and with a clear-mind, without its help.

• Work at your meditation with daily diligence, and you'll find that its benefits will begin to spread into all aspects of your life.

• If your meditation is honest and genuine, these benefits will include humility. Humility isn't a false modesty or "putting yourself down." Humility is really the same thing as honesty: *seeing yourself as you really are*. True humility is *accepting yourself to the point that you can let the self go completely*, seeing yourself only in terms of what we've called personalism.

• Your enemies are laziness, parasites and everything that feeds them.

• Let what you learn in meditation carry over into every aspect of your relations with others.

Step Two: Believe

"Whether you become a great shaman or just a bloke that can talk to his ancestors, you will have an expanded mind and will be able to dream (*make real, PFE*) many things," Mindiluwi said.

Taking the step from simply accepting the multiverse to actually believing in it will give you potential and power for just about anything, in union with the rest of us. Once you have the power of belief, you will begin to experience a new depth to things and to people. Your experience of life will expand dramatically. You will find yourself less drawn to the incessant distractions modern life dangles before us, and more drawn to things that really matter in the multiverse – other people, the

Earth, your own potential, our common destiny to realize we're divine.

Most crucially, the artificial differences between people and things will begin to blur. You will begin to see people, things and even your daily tasks not according to pigeonholes, labels and categories, but as unique and necessary parts of the whole.

You will begin to experience the Unity. And you will begin to see God.

Accepting cleared the way for you to climb high enough to see, and start experiencing, the multiverse. *Believing* what you have accepted will clear the way for you to take an active role in it, for yourself and for all of us. Belief, like falling in love, is a true act of the will. Belief gives you power because belief means knowledge. It means you know not only where you are and what you're doing. It means *you can access knowledge and abilities you have elsewhere and elsewhen in the multiverse.*

Depending on how well you've connected with yourself, you have become twice, three times, ten times, a hundred times the person you were. But, as we've said, we are at a point on our evolution where we can handle only so much exposure to our own subconscious. *If you feel yourself being carried away or overwhelmed at any point, STOP and regroup.* You may not be meant to go any further yet.

"I've seen a few great shamans come from among your people, but it's hard for them because they have to change everything about how they think. Sometimes they can't handle it," Mindiluwi pointed out. "A few have ended in hospitals or babbling on street corners, up a gumtree (*in a mess, PFE*). No matter what people we are, white or *binghi* (*aborigines as our older brothers, PFE*), we can't bite off more than we can chew."

Step Three: Act

"Your people need a lot of help. They don't know where they

are, what they're doing, or why they're on the Earth," Mindiluwi cautioned. "They can't dream, but they have to learn to. Any one of your people that expands his mind into the Dream Time has to help the others. If they don't, the whole human race won't make it."

Once you possess the power of belief and have begun to recover the Unity, your greatest happiness will be in experiencing and spreading it. It will be time to use what you know. It will be time to act.

Having tied into the best energies of your more enlightened self from other parts of the multiverse, you'll find another paradox: Sometimes the best way to act is *not* to act: Sometimes the best policy is, "let it be." *Let your subconscious guide you; your total self knows best.*

• Make no conscious plans for the future; they may be wrong because your conscious mind can't see the big picture. Let your subconscious guide you. As doors close, turn away from them. As doors open, walk through them. Deal with things as they arise. As the need shows itself, act. As you see, judge. It's another paradox: Take each day as it comes, with love, openness and energy, and you'll be amazed where you'll go and what you'll accomplish!

• All this about not being judgmental is nonsense. It will be your duty to judge, especially if you're a parent, with your expanded perspective in the multiverse. Be aware that our enemies in the multiverse include evil people who can harm you, your family and all of us. Just as you will have learned to connect with your better selves in the multiverse, the evil person will not have learned to disconnect himself or herself from negative selves.

• At the same time, temper your judgments, your actions and your thoughts with compassion for all people and all things. Remember that you share the lives even of the parasites. In all things, love.

"Love seems to be a problem for your people," Mindiluwi pointed out. "You don't seem to know anything about it. You think it means liking somebody a lot, or you think it means sex. I was at my son's house last week, and my grandchildren were watching *Star Trek*. That *alf* (*dummy, PFE*) with the ears who is supposed to be so smart? He says love is an emotion. Love is the way you live your life, the way you dream your life and the whole world!"

Love is a state of being that takes its soul from the Unity. So much for Mr. Spock.

As Mindiluwi suggested, we are so individualistic that we don't even know what love is except in applying it to ourselves. Our relationships, marriages and families fall apart because we don't love each other; we love ourselves *through* each other. Our relationships are a sort of shared loneliness.

"People have to be careful to treat each other right. When you get mad and swear at somebody, and get them upset, you're hurting most of all yourself. You're hurting the whole world," Mindiluwi stated.

Go out of your way to be cheerful, to make someone smile every day, to uplift people's spirits. Cultivate kindness; it's contagious. This will help draw everyone you encounter toward the Unity. The Unity can teach us the power and the meaning of love because, to get there, we have to truly forget the self. And you cannot love unless you do that.

• Acting in your expanded life will include awareness of, and perhaps communication with, your ancestors and passed loved ones without having to resort to questionable people and practices, such as storefront mediums or, God forbid, Ouija boards and séances (never use these!).

Even before you expand your life, you will be able to help and heal your loved ones, or even strangers, who have passed from this world to others, and who may need this help. As we've said, some mediums would have you believe that any loved one who passes on automatically becomes a guardian. This isn't so. As I've seen in my own work, some of them need more help than we do because their consciousness may have shifted to a not-so-great world.

Christian denominations that pray for the dead draw that practice from a very old theological concept: We pray for the dead because *it can help them in their lives*. If that's not a concept right out of multiverse awareness, there is no such thing!

We all cry for our departed loved ones. It's a natural reaction to that empty place at the table, and the one in our hearts. But your loved ones are *not* dead, any more than we are because we're "dead" in a some parallel worlds. Your relationships with these people simply change. You still feel them in the places and with the people they loved, and still love. They and you are always there in close parallel worlds that often occupy the same space. Relish their presence and, if they are in a position to offer it, their quiet help and guidance. If you love someone — anywhere or anywhen – you're always in union with them, and all you have to do is listen.

Once in awhile, however, it's just time to say goodbye. Don't hold onto them when they're in a world that demands other tasks from them. Don't worry: You'll know.

All relationships take hard work, especially in this digital world. I think that the more gadgets we have to help us communicate, the less we know *how* to communicate. That goes for everyday family relationships and ongoing relationships with those whose awareness has joined them in a parallel world. If you're a praying person, here's a place to start: When you pray for your loved ones, pray for the living and the "dead" together, not separately. And include *all* your ancestors, most of whose names you won't even know. This can help them wherever or whenever they are, and it will begin to awaken your whole understanding of life and the non-existence of death in the multiverse.

• You may be able to heal yourself and others of physical disease by making real in this world a world where the disease never occurred. But healing is best done by people as a group.

• A very important part of your action will be helping others in our own conscious world, especially those who will be drawn to you, and many will find you attractive, even charismatic, after you have expanded your life. You, in turn, will be drawn to others who are discovering the Unity.

This is important, because learning to act as a community again is crucial to human destiny. The more multiverse-connected, positive people who come together, the more action can be taken to pull all humanity, and the planet, away from negative energy.

Remember myth and folklore? Many of our everyday actions, especially actions of faith, recall ancient beliefs about our group effectiveness in the multiverse.

• Do you pray for others or ask them to pray for you? You're not only calling on God, you're using the power of your mind and your love to reach out for a world where the person's need doesn't exit, and striving to make it real in our conscious world. You're using the multiverse!

• When is the last time you hugged someone? We frequently do so as a "hello" or "goodbye" (the latter coming from the Middle English for "God be with you"). Hugging descends in direct line from our hunter-gatherer ancestors, who expressed good feeling and wishes for friends' and relatives' well-being against the elements by sharing body heat. But it's also a symbol of holding a loved one in the same world as we are, where he or she will be safe.

• Holding hands: It's sharing warmth and affection, of course, but it's also sharing power.

Sharing and combining our power within the multiverse really starts clicking when we act as a group. When I teach a family to come together, hold hands and build up positive energy against a parasite attack, I'm teaching them to use their multiverse power for defense.

When the good folks on that West Virginia ghost walk in 2003 came together to send love to the suffering Margaret Blennerhasset, we were using the power of the multiverse to send love and share power with a fellow creature in another world.

• New Agers tout the "power of visualization," and this is one of the things they're right about. From visualizing yourself in a brilliant white light as a defense against parasites, to a group of meditators visualizing someone healed of an illness, it works. Much like prayer, visualization sends the power of human minds into the multiverse to connect with worlds where the desired possibility already exists. It can cause the worlds to blend, making the miracle real.

A convention of the Transcendental Meditation® program once met in Providence, Rhode Island, when I was an editor at that city's daily newspaper. Our stories made much of the fact that the convention-goers spent a great deal of time "meditating for peace." While this drew snickers from people all over the state, there was an immediate and noticeable calming of world conflicts, and a rise in peace initiatives, over the ensuing month. It was so noticeable that it drew comment in the newsroom and was, in my opinion, "statistically significant"!

Can you imagine the affect of thousands of people "meditating for peace" all over the world – or perhaps all over the worlds?

Shaking the Multiverse

It's no exaggeration to say that the world's people are in dire need of the love, cooperation and understanding only the Unity can bring. But we also are in dire need of defense.

As we build up our power as people and as a species, we can't forget that parasites and other possible enemies not only share the multiverse with us, they've done us great harm in the past. Parasites, especially, can have no desire to see us coming together, and lessening our output of negative energy. They can have no desire to see us cut off their food supply.

I know first-hand that parasites aren't stupid; quite the contrary. Not to be paranoid about it, but I can't help but wonder what influence these creatures may have in the halls of government, what "buttons" they can push with the world's leaders, political, economic and military. With the world becoming increasingly "smaller" and more globalized, it also becomes increasingly dangerous. Terrorists seem able to hit targets anywhere with relative impunity. Nuclear, biological and chemical weapons are proliferating beyond control. Famine, poverty and civil disorder can strike anywhere, especially in a global economy in which the whole world population pretty much stands or falls together.

Well, you might say, if the whole world goes *kaboom*, won't we all just wake up in a similar world in the multiverse and just pick up where we left off, and be none the wiser?

Probably, but is that such a fabulous prospect, especially being none the wiser?

We've said that everything we are and everything we do echoes across the worlds. We don't need the kind of negativity that's in our conscious world now, or the kind of catastrophes that are hanging close by in parallel worlds.

We need to clear out the negative energy as much as we can at this stage in our evolution, and we need to take the next step – taking charge of our own divine destiny in the multiverse by working together in the Unity.

We must make the multiverse ring with love, or we must

perish together. We must, as Mindiluwi said, become "one tribe, one blood."

Final Thoughts

What is it that makes us human? Being *homo sapiens sapiens*, knowing that we know, means knowing the multiverse. I don't think we've become fully human even yet.

As they gazed at the beauty of the moon and stars, held each other's hands before the miracles of birth and death, or huddled together in terror of the thunder, our distant forbears asked questions. As they looked silently from the African hilltops at the glory of the sunset, they asked "How?" As they watched their kin die between the teeth of the beast, they asked "Why?" As they watched life bloom in the spring, they said "Wow!"

When they dreamed strange dreams, they wondered. When they saw the faces of their lost loved ones in the dark, or felt the gods of the savannah or woodland, or thanked the spirits of their prey during the hunt, they knew there was far more to the world than met the eye. From day one, we as a species wanted – thirsted – to explain the unexplained. And in the unexplained – in the paranormal – we discovered our Primal God.

That was our true beginning.

Because they apparently had the good sense to realize that their quiver of knowledge was pretty slim, the first thing the first human ancestors must have realized was that alone is not good. Alone you find less food, you have to work harder for a smaller result, you are colder and more afraid of the dark. Alone you are in more danger from predators and the elements. Alone you are lonesome.

Alone you die.

According to evolutionary theory and anthropology, we must already have known this when we were still swinging from the trees by our prehensile toes. Our apparent simian forebears got together early. Pairs became families. Families became tribes. Individuals became irrelevant.

We learned that we could achieve a great deal more together than we ever could alone. Even then, we felt the holes in our souls, and we began to strive again for the Unity.

Even greed could feed the desire for the Unity.

Whether prodded by "intruders" or not, the most powerful kings and warlords reached out from their cities and started to build nations and empires. They strove to unify people once more, albeit often with violence and cruelty.

The Akkadians, Babylonians, Egyptians and Romans were but a few. The Romans were by far the most successful in uniting Europe, North Africa and the Middle East, and their example has been the model for all Western unifiers and would-be unifiers -- and sometimes tyrants -- ever since. Queen Elizabeth I, Napoleon and Hitler all admired the Romans. The unifying instinct still goes on in Europe through the European Union.

Even tribalism and racism are wayward attempts at the unification instinct. But as soon as we get to know people personally, share with them, experience hardship or plenty with them, our and their defenses break down, and they usually become part of our tribe. No matter how different they are, they no longer seem alien.

In every nook and cranny of history, we find examples of sincere, or blundering, or misguided, or simply wrong examples of people trying to unify.

The Romans didn't persecute Christians because the former were enraged by Jesus and His message. They persecuted Christians because the latter wouldn't participate fully in society, especially by sacrificing to the emperor, the ultimate symbol of unity to the Romans. The Romans thought the Christians undermined the unity of the human race.

The Unity remains elusive today because we have little sense of dependence on one another. Even families seem to have trouble staying together. We look inside ourselves when we should look beyond, not realizing that we already have the Unity. It never left us; we left It.

Down deep, we all have two questions: Are my departed loved ones okay? In the end, will I be okay?

We have our answers. Let's turn home.

May we do so now, and as "one tribe, one blood." And may this be celebrated by our remote ancestors and descendants across infinity. May it be shouted from the towers of a trillion worlds: That in this, our world, we were the generation who came together, became gods and goddesses, and brought back the Unity. We were the ones to reveal God once again.

May we be able to whisper to our own newborn children: "Welcome! Welcome to this good, this holy, this right, this true world. Welcome home!"

Acknowledgments

My first thanks go to a man who never knew me: Dr. Dan Q. Posin (1910-2003), former professor of physics at DePaul University, Chicago. Refugee from the Russian Revolution, prolific author, and tireless campaigner for world peace in the nuclear age, Dr. Posin was a friend of Albert Einstein, who told him that he had a unique gift for explaining science to children.

I was one of those children. At 4 o'clock every afternoon in the early 1960s I would tune in to a show on what was then the new National Educational Television network to see where in the universe this little man with the big mustache was going to take me that day. "Dr. Dan" would dance around the set, providing sound effects for model spaceships, to visit other planets, numerous stars, and what promised to be a golden future. Sometimes his cat, Minerva, would be with him.

Dr. Dan Q. Posin was truly the rocket power for my own early love of science, and I know scientists today who say he did the same for them when they were kids. I'm not sure what he would have thought of the ideas in this book, but I know he would have embraced at least one: That golden future, if only humankind will choose it.

For his kind permission to use photos from his Middle East and India trip, taken when he "was a lot younger," many thanks to my old friend Steve Hitchins. Thanks also to my newer friend, Donna Fillie, for use of her photos. Also, for their kind cooperation in the photo department, Lebanon's Ministry of Tourism and West Virginia's Division of Natural Resources.

Thanks also to my wife and sons for their patience as I spent most of the past year in my study writing this book!

Bibliography

AUERBACH, Loyd. *ESP, Hauntings and Poltergeists: A Parapsychologist's Handbook*. New York: Warner Books, 1986.

BARNES, Jonathan. *Early Greek Philosophy*. New York: Penguin Books, 1987.

BECKER, Robert O. and SELDEN, Gary. *The Body Electric: Electromagnetism and the Foundation of Life*. New York: William Morrow, 1985.

BROOKESMITH, Peter (Ed.). *Thinking the Unthinkable: Ideas which have Upset Conventional Thought*. London: Orbis Publishing, 1980.

BUCK, William (Ed.). *The Mahabharata*. Berkeley: University of California Press, 1973.

BUDGE, E.A. Wallis. *Legends of the Egyptian Gods: Hieroglyphic Texts ad Translations*. New York: Dover Publications, 1994.

BURENHULT, Goran (Ed.). *The First Humans: Human Origins and History to 10,000 BC*. San Francisco: Harper & Row, 1993.

CAMPBELL, Joseph (Ed.). *Myths, Dreams and Religion*. Dallas: Spring Publications, 1970.

CAMPBELL, Joseph. *The Power of Myth*. New York: Anchor Books, 1991.

CANER, Ergun Mehmet. *Unveiling Islam: An Insider's Look at Muslim Life and Beliefs*. Grand Rapids, Mich.: Kregel Publications, 2002.

CAPRA, Fritjof. *The Tao of Physics: An Exploration of the Parallels between Modern Physics and Eastern Mysticism*. Berkeley, Calif.: Shambhala, 1975.

CLARKE, Graham. *World Prehistory in a New Perspective*. London: Cambridge University Press, 1977.

COLEMAN, Loren. *Mysterious America (Revised Edition)*. New York: Paraview Press, 2001.

COTT, Jonathan. *The Search for Omm Sety: Reincarnation and Eternal Love*. Garden City, N.Y.: Doubleday, 1987.

CREMO, Michael A. and THOMPSON, Richard L. *Forbidden Archaeology: The Hidden History of the Human Race*. Los Angeles: Bhaktivedanta Book Publishing, 1993.

DEUTSCH, David. *The Fabric of Reality*. New York: Penguin Books, 1997.

ELKIN, A.P. *Aboriginal Men of High Degree: Initiation and Sorcery in the World's Oldest Tradition*. Rochester, Vt.: Inner Traditions, 1993.

ENO, Paul F. *Faces at the Window: First-Hand Accounts of the Paranormal in Southern New England*. Woonsocket, R.I.: New River Press, 1998.

ENO, Paul F. *Footsteps in the Attic: More First-Hand Accounts of the Paranormal in New England*. Woonsocket, R.I.: New River Press, 2002.

ENO, Robert B. *Saint Augustine and the Saints*. Villanova, Pa.: Villanova University Press, 1989.

ENO, Robert B. (Tr.). *The Fathers of the Church: St. Augustine Letters*. Washington: The Catholic University of America Press, 1989.

EHRMAN, Bart D. *Misquoting Jesus: The Story Behind Who Changed the Bible and Why*. San Francisco: Harper Collins, 2005.

FLOROVSKY, Georges. *Bible, Church, Tradition: An Eastern Orthodox View*. Belmont, Mass.: Nordland Publishing Co., 1972.

FLOROVSKY, Georges. *Creation and Redemption.*. Belmont, Mass.: Nordland Publishing Co., 1976.

FORT, Charles. *The Complete Books of Charles Fort*. New York: Dover Publications, 1974.

FOX, Robin Lane. *Pagans and Christians*. New York: Alfred A. Knopf, 1987.

FRANKFORT, Henri. *Kingship and the Gods: A Study of Ancient Near Eastern Religion as the Integration of Society and Nature.* Chicago: University of Chicago Press, 1948.

GIMBUTAS, Marija. *The Language of the Goddess.* New York: Harper & Row, 1989.

GOLB, Norman. *Who Wrote the Dead Sea Scrolls?: The Search for the Secret of Qumran.* New York: Scribner, 1995.

GOSWAMI, Amit. *The Self-Aware Universe: How Consciousness Creates the Material World.* New York: G.P. Putnam's Sons, 1993.

GOULD, Stephen Jay. *Wonderful Life· The Burgess Shale and the Nature of History.* New York: W.W. Norton & Co., 1989.

GRIBBIN, John. *In Search of Schroedinger's Cat: Quantum Physics and Reality.* New York: Bantam Books, 1984.

HANCOCK, Graham. *Fingerprints of the Gods: The Evidence of Earth's Lost Civilization.* New York: Random House, 1995.

HARNER, Michael. *The Way of the Shaman.* New York: Bantam Books, 1980.

HEENAN, Edward F. (Ed.). *Mystery, Magic and Miracle: Religion in a Post-Aquarian Age.* Englewood Cliffs, N.J.: Prentice-Hall, 1973.

HERBERT, Nick. *Quantum Reality: Beyond the New Physics.* Garden City, N.Y.: Doubleday, 1985.

HEIDEGGER, Martin. *Being and Time (Sein Und Zeit).* San Francisco: Harper & Row, 1962.

HONDERICH, Ted (Ed.). *The Oxford Companion to Philosophy.* New York: Oxford University Press, 1995.

HOYLE, Fred. *The Intelligent Universe.* New York: Holt, Rinehart and Winston, 1983.

INGERSOLL, Robert Green. *Complete works of Robert Green Ingersoll Online.* http://www.infidels.org/library/historical/robert_ingersoll/

JOHANSON, Donald and MAITLAND, Edey. Lucy: The Beginnings of Mankind. New York: Warner Books, 1981.

KANE, Dave. *41 Signs of Hope*. Woonsocket, R.I.: New River Press, 2006.

KEEL, John A. *The Complete Guide to Mysterious Beings*. New York: Tor Books, 1970.

KEEL, John A. *The Mothman Prophecies*. New York: Tor Books, 1975.

KEEL, John A. *Our Haunted Planet*. Lakeville, Minn.: Galde Press, 2002.

KOSAMBI, D.D. *Ancient India: A History of Its Culture and Civilization*. Cleveland: Meridian Books, 1965.

KRAEMER, Ross Shepard. *Her Share of the Blessings: Women's Religions Among Pagans, Jews and Christians in the Greco-Roman World*. New York: Oxford University Press, 1992.

LASCH, Christopher. *The Culture of Narcissism: American Life in an Age of Diminishing Expectations*. New York: Warner Books, 1979.

LEAKEY, Richard and LEWIN, Roger. *Origins Reconsidered: In Search of What Makes Us Human*. New York: Doubleday, 1992.

LEIGH, Julia and SAVOLD, David. *The Day that Lightning Chased the Housewife...And Other Mysteries of Science*. New York: Madison Books, 1988.

LOWITH, Karl. *Meaning in History*. Chicago: University of Chicago Press, 1949.

MANITONQUAT. *Return to Creation*. Spokane, Wash.: Bear Tribe Publishing, 1991.

MILLER, Patricia Cox. *Dreams in Late Antiquity: Studies in the Imagination of a Culture*. Princeton, N.J.: Princeton University Press, 1994.

MOORE, Thomas. *The Re-Enchantment of Everyday Life*. New York: Harper Collins, 1996.

NASR, Seyyed Hossein. *Islam: Religion, History, Civilization*. New York: Harper Collins, 2003.

O'BRIEN, Christian. *The Genius of the Few*. Gloucestershire: Dianthus Publishing Ltd., 1985.

PELIKAN, Jaroslav. *The World Treasury of Modern Religious Thought*. Boston: Little, Brown and Company, 1990.

PETREMENT, Simone. *A Separate God: The Christian Origins of Gnosticism*. San Francisco: Harper & Row, 1984.

POSIN, Dan Q. *I Have Been to the Village*. Ann Arbor, Mich.: Edwards Brothers, 1948.

POSIN, Dan Q. *Out of This World*. Chicago: Popular Mechanics Press, 1959.

RHINE, Joseph B. *Extrasensory Perception* (revised edition). Boston: Bruce Humphries, 1973.

RHINE, Joseph B. *New Frontiers of the Mind: The Story of the Duke Experiments*. New York: Farrar & Rinehart, 1937.

RHINE, Louisa E. *Hidden Channels of the Mind*. New York: William Morrow and Co., 1961.

SACHS, Robert G. *The Physics of Time Reversal*. Chicago: University of Chicago Press, 1987.

SAGAN, Carl and PAGE, Thornton. *UFO's: A Scientific Debate*. New York: Barnes and Noble Books, 1972.

SITCHIN, Zecharia. *Genesis Revisited: Is Modern Science Catching Up with Ancient Knowledge?* New York: Avon Books, 1990.

SHERMER, Michael. *Why People Believe Weird Things: Pseudoscience, Superstition and Other Confusions of Our Time*. New York: W.H. Freeman and Co., 1997.

TILLICH, Paul. *A History of Christian Thought from its Judaic and Hellenistic Origins to Existentialism*. New York: Harper & Row, 1967.

VALLEE, Jacques. *Forbidden Science*. New York, Marlowe & Co., 1992.

VAN DOREN, Charles. *A History of Knowledge: The Pivotal Events, People and Achievements of World History*. New York: Ballantine Books, 1991.

VIOLETTE, John R. *Extra Dimensional Universe*. Charlottesville, Va.: Hampton Roads Publishing, 2001.

WATSON, Lyall. *Gifts of Unknown Things.* New York: Simon and Schuster, 1976.

WEINTRAUB, Pamela (Ed.). *Omni's Catalog of the Bizarre.* New York: Doubeday, 1985.

WHITE, Rhea A. *Parapsychology.* Lanham, Md.: Scarecrow Press, 1991.

WILSON, Colin. *The Encyclopedia of Unsolved Mysteries.* New York: Contemporary Books, 1987.

WILSON, Colin and GRANT, John. *The Directory of Possibilities.* New York: The Rutledge Press, 1981.

WOLF, Fred Alan. *Star Wave: Mind, Consciousness and Quantum Physics.* New York: Macmillan Publishing Co., 1984.

WOLMAN, Benjamin B. (Ed.). *Handbook of Parapsychology.* New York: Van Nostrand Reinhold Co., 1977.

ZELDIN, Theodore. *An Intimate History of Humanity.* London: Reed Consumer Books, 1994.

Sacred Scriptures

The Jerusalem Bible (The Torah—Hebrew Edition). Jerusalem: Koren Publishers, 1992.

The New English Bible (The New Testament). London: Oxford University Press, Cambridge University Press, 1970.

The Qur'an. Princeton, N.J.: Princeton University Press, 1988.

The Dhammapada. London: Oxford University Press, 1987.

The Rig Veda. Delhi, India: Motilal Banarsidass Publishers, 1992.

The Tanakh. Philadelphia: The Jewish Publication Society, 1985.

The Bhagavad Gita. Baltimore: Penguin Books, 1962.

Index

Aborigines 183; concept of guruwari
193, 194, 195; Mindiluwi
194, 195, 197, 198, 199, 200, 201, 206; oral history
93, 94
Abraham 147, 148
Adonai 147
Africa 94; monotheism in 93; Zambia 127
Agnosticism 71, 75
Air Force, U.S. 141
Akas: oral history 93
Akkadians 128, 130, 136, 138, 207
Allah 149
American Society for Psychical Research (ASPR) 17, 18, 46
American Society for Psychical, The Journal of the 41
An American Haunting: 2006 film 114, 116
Ancestors 18, 198, 206; as guardians
155, 162, 163, 172, 197
Ancestors, honoring: Chinese neopaganism 76
Andaman and Nicobar Islands: natives of: oral traditions 94
Angels
24, 105, 129, 145, 146, 148, 149, 150, 187, 197; fallen
132
Annunage 129, 130
Anthropology 102, 119, 121, 206
Anthropomorphism 94
Anu 131, 136, 183; as "The Most High" 129
Aphrodite, Goddess 117
Apollo, God 179
Arabs 92; Muslim and Christian 73
Archaeology

81, 91, 102, 112, 119, 129, 135, 136; processual approach 121
Aristotle 21, 81, 189
Armenia 127
Asia 104, 117, 127; bizarre fossils 125; monotheism in 93
Assyrians 92
Astrobiology 107
Athanasius the Great, St. 188
Atheism, atheists 74, 75, 184; as a religion 71
Athena, Goddess 182, 188
Atra-Hasis 128, 130, 141, 183
Australia 192; Melbourne 193; monotheism in 93
Aztecs: oral history 93

Babylonians 92, 136, 207
Baiame, God 181, 183
Bara Hack 13, 14, 16, 24, 26, 28, 29, 30, 31, 32, 45
Belief: as act of will 199
Bell Family 114
Berbers: oral history 93
Berry, Dr. Daniel M. 97
Bhagavad Gita 185
Bhagavad-Gita 96
Bible, The
  22, 23, 97, 98, 114, 127, 130, 132, 146, 148, 189; flying vehicles in 134
Big Bang, The 84
Bigfoot 16, 124; photography 126
Biology 122
Biosphere 85, 88, 90, 164, 192; as spanning multiverse 89; as superorganism 89
Blennerhassett, Margaret 63, 64, 204
Bradbury, Ray 20
Brain waves 108
Brigit 182
British Broadcasting Corporation 71
British Museum 116
Brown, Dr. Frank 34, 50
Bruno, Giordano 185
Buddha, The 117, 179
Buddhism, Buddhists: and non-belief in God 79; and reincarnation 167; belief in angels 145; Mahayana tradition 79

Burke, Sir Edmund 160
Bushmen 94, 97

Callimachus 188
Canaanites 92, 128
Capra, Dr. Fritjof 40, 41
Caribs: oral history 93
Chaldeans 92
Chaos Theory: and crop circles 154; and fractals 89
Charbonneau, Rev. William 35
Chariots of the Gods 119
Children: terminally ill: as other-centered 163
China 41; atheism in 71
Christianity, Christians
    22, 23, 79, 97, 98, 113, 148, 149; adoption of pagan
    feasts 179; as a form of paganism 80; belief in angels
    145; early: and reincarnation 168; helping Muslims
    129; mainstream denominations: declining in developed
    nations 76; Old Testament 97; persecuted by Romans
    207; prayers for the dead 202
Clairaudience 7
Clairvoyance 7
Coast Guard, U.S. 33
College St-Michel 120
Colorado 158
Connecticut 55, 162; Bloomfield 13; Bridgeport 30; Cov-
    entry 30; East Hartford 13, 32; Hartford 35; New Britain
    30; New Haven 30; Pomfret 11; Tolland 35
Council of the Gods 130
Crop circles 154
Cryptids 7, 86

Dallas Morning News 176
Darwin, Charles 74, 85
Death: as absence of life 161; as easy out 171; as nonexistent
    159, 161, 164, 165, 203; process 171; violent 60
Déjà vu 7
Demonology 31
Demons 32, 36, 39, 40, 45, 49, 50, 57, 104, 112
Denominations and sects: intermarriage 73
Descartes, Rene 21
Devas 145

Devil, The 30; existence of 141; Iblis 142; Mainyu 142; Satan 142; servants of 105
Diana, Goddess 182
Dickens, Charles 16
Diet: as meditation tool 196
Dissociative identity disorder 34
Divine Child 96
DNA: deoxyribonucleic acid 85, 86, 94; genetic engineering 130, 139; genetic record 90; mystery genes 122
Doctors, medical: as believers in God 72
Dogons: oral history 93
Dover Demon 124
Dream: as creative force 95, 193, 198; as warning 156
Dream Time 94, 96, 112, 118, 150, 182, 183, 193, 200
Dreher, Rod 176

Earth: as mother 96
Easter Island 120
Eastern Orthodox Church 181; ethnic affiliations 74; phyletism 74; theology of miracles 150
Eden, Ehden 129; Garden of Eden 129
Edison, Thomas 120
Egypt 117, 181, 207; Dendera 77; monotheism in 93
Einstein, Dr. Albert 185
El Shaddai 131; as "The Most High" 129
Electrical fields 89, 107, 109; affect on animals 66; affect on cameras 126; direct current 34, 50; polarity reversal 62, 64
Electroencephalograph 108
Electromagnetism 50, 65, 164; as cause of crop circles 154; EMF meter 51, 52, 53, 56, 62; geomagnetic fields 52; used by parasites 111
electromagnetism: as cause for religious experience 184
Electronic voice phenomena: EVP 155
Electropollution 65, 154; as hindrance to meditation 196; microwaves 52, 109
Elohim 128, 130, 146
Energy: negative 107, 112, 197, 203, 205; as attracting parasites 61; defined 61; positive 111, 204; as weapon against parasites 61; defined 61
England: West Country 83
Enlightenment: as escape from reincarnation 169, 172

Enlightenment, The 14, 15, 16
Enlil 129, 136, 140, 142, 148; as Sky God 92
Enoch 132
Enoch, Book of 132
Environmental crisis 186
Epilepsy, temporal lobe 33
Epypt 136
Eriugena, John Scotus 185
Essenes: and reincarnation 168
Ethnicism: in religion 73
Everett, Dr. Hugh 41
Evolution, theory of 74, 98, 206; and genetic mystery 122
Exceptional human experiences 7, 89, 104
Exorcism 31, 35
Extra-sensory perception (ESP) 7, 17, 18

Fasting: explained 196
Folklore: (see *also* Myth) 81, 93, 102
Fossil record 90
Fractals 89, 164, 193, 194
Frankfort, Dr. Henri 92, 102, 112

Gabriel, Archangel 148
Gaia Theory 88, 95, 98, 166
Geotechnics 109
Germany, Munich 34
Ghostbusters, 1984 film 20
Gnostics 168
God: as alien 182; as cosmic vending machine 73, 180; as
    different in New Testament 80, 148; as Elohim 128; as
    First Fractal 95; as Heart of the Unity 96; as living in the
    sky 138; as middle class 180; as Mother: absent from
    modern religions 181; Baiame 94; Huve 94, 97; known
    by experience 175; male and female principles
    95, 140, 148; our Primal God 90, 93-96
    98, 99, 112, 113, 139, 140, 142, 146, 148, 150, 176, 188; as
    "Alpha Point" 80; as Divine Female 181; as found in the
    paranormal 206; humans as fractals of 89; return of
    87; Paluga 94; questions about 6; secret name of 147
Goswami, Dr. Amit 41, 161
Greece 117
Guenon, Rene 186

Gutenberg, Johannes 22

Hammurabi 136; law code of 137
Hancock, Graham 81, 96
Hathor 182
Hathor, Goddess: as "mother of all children" 77
Heaven 29, 173
Heaven's Gate cult 160
Hebrew 128, 146, 176, 189
Hegel, Georg 185
Helder, Luke J. 158, 160, 171
Hell 29; as being in the Earth 138; nature of 172
Herbert, Dr. Nick 41
Hinduism, Hindus: and reincarnation 167; as polytheistic
    79; belief in angels 145; Bhagavad-Gita 96, 97
History 119, 121; as fractals 89; cyclical theory of 81; linear
    theory of 81
Holy Spirit: feminine characteristics 97
Holy Trinity 80, 97, 148, 149, 175, 176
Holzer, Dr. Hans 27
Homo Adorans 96
Homo sapiens 96, 206
Hoyle, Sir Fred 104, 122
Human Genome Project 122
Human mind: subconscious: as vessel of race memory 82
Humility: defined 198
Huve, God 181

Iamblichus 188
Illinois 158; bizarre fossils 125
Illinois, Chicago 35
Illinois, Evanston 34
India 41, 136; as home of Jainism 79; Epic of
    134, 135; monotheism in 93
Individualism 15, 112, 118, 161, 187; vs. personalism
    87, 90
Indo-European language group 138, 150
Ingersoll, Robert G. 178, 179, 182
Inuits: oral history 93
Iowa 158
Iraq: excavations in 92

Isaac 147
Isaiah the Prophet 97
Isis, Goddess 77, 179, 182; as Mother of the World
    117, 181
Israel: Hebron 113
Iulianus, Flavius Claudius 188

Jainism, Jains: and non-belief in God 79; and reincarnation
    167, 168
Jersey Devil 124
Jesus Christ 23, 149, 207; as ascending into heaven 138; as
    destroyer of death 169; as possible Essene 168; as Son of
    Man 98; as Sun of Righteousness 179
Jibril: Malaikah 149
Judaism, Jews 22, 23, 79, 80, 97, 142, 148; and reincarna-
    tion 167; belief in angels 145; Holocaust 113; Shekinah
    97

Kabbalah 167
Karma 164
Keel, John A. 140, 141
Kentucky: bizarre fossils 125; Hopkinsville 153
Kenya: Rift Valley 132
Kharsag 129, 140, 142, 148
Kharsag Epics 128, 141, 183
Khwe: oral history 93
Krishna 135, 179

Langdon, Dr. Stephen H. 91, 92
Lao Tze 185
Larivee, Sr. Rita 72, 187
Lebanon: Qadisha Valley 131, 133; "Holy Valley" 129; Rift
    Valley 132
Loch Ness Monster 124
Lords of Cultivation 128
Love 60; as a state of being 201; as act of will 199
Lovelock, Dr. James E. 88

Magonians 153
Mahabharata, The 134, 135, 141
Maine, York Harbor 36, 39, 46

Malachi, Prophet 179
Malaikah 148
Marshall, Bishop John A. 31
Maryam 149
Masai: oral history 93
Massachusetts 48; Boston 166; Northbridge 66; Uxbridge
    51; West Springfield 30
Max Planck Institute 34
Maximus the Confessor, St. 188
Meditation 159; as tool for acceptance 194; technique
    196, 197; using a mantra 196, 198
Mediums 17, 28, 32, 46, 86, 113, 151, 201, 202; as
    ignorant about multiverse 170; in Roman Catholic Church
    78
Mind: subconscious: as guide in life 200
Miracles: and angels 150; defined 150
Mitochondria 90
Mohenjo Daro 136, 137
Monotheism 91, 92; as predating polytheism 91
Mormonism, Mormons: belief in angels 145
Moses 23
Mothman 124, 140
Mothman Prophecies, The 140
Mound Builders 115, 116
Mt. Ida College 166
Muhammed, the Prophet 23, 148
Muhammedanism, Muslims 22, 80, 113, 148, 149; and
    pantheism 186; as monotheistic 77; Bektashis 73; belief
    in angels 145; Harufis 73; honoring Jesus Christ
    79; Shiites 73; Sufis 73; helping Christians 129; Sunnis
    73
Multiverse 43-45,
    47, 48, 55, 64, 71, 72, 95, 105, 111, 112, 119, 140, 149; anal-
    ogy of 164; and paradoxes 85; and simultaneous lives
    167; and subconscious mind 82; and time 167; as a unified
    system 86; as blueprint for reality 95, 126; as explosion of
    divine love 84; as paradox 86; drop-ins from 124; intrud-
    ers from 123, 130, 133, 134, 138; parallel worlds
    45, 46, 50, 57, 58, 60, 62, 103, 124, 126, 140, 146, 191; health
    hazards 65; shared lives in 165, 166; using the
    152, 195; worlds as fractals 89
Myth 99, 103, 104, 127, 133, 167, 203; and reincarnation

172; as evidence 93; as vessel of memory
94, 109, 123, 132, 146; modern 153

National Catholic Reporter 72
Native Americans 116
Neanderthal man 127
Near-death experiences 7, 24
Nebraska 158
Neopaganism 76, 142
Neuroscience, cognitive 108
Nevada: Reno 159
New Age, The 23, 76, 77, 159, 181, 182; and environmental
crisis 88; and pantheism 186; and reIncarnation
168; spirituality 160
New Brunswick: Dieppe 70
New Testament 138, 149; 1 Corinthians 170; Acts of the
Apostles 138; and eternal punishment 178; Luke, Gospel
of 138; Matthew, Gospel of 167
New York: Cortland 30; New York 34; Ogdensburg 33
Newton, Sir Isaac 74; laws of motion 74
Nietzsche, Friedrich 21
Nigeria 71
Ninkharsag 129, 140, 182
Ninlil 129, 140, 182; as Mother Goddess 130, 138
Noah 132
North America: monotheism in 93
North Carolina: Dunn 153
North Korea: atheism in 71
Northwestern University 34
Norwich State Hospital 33
Nuclear weapons 135

O'Brien, Christian 122, 123
Odin, God: worship of 76
Ogdensburg State Hospital 33
Ohio 64, 140
Ohio River 63, 124, 140
Old Testament: Genesis, Book of 122, 128, 141, 146, 181
Omega Point 98
Ontario: Ottawa 36, 39, 46
Osiris, God 179; as Father of the World 117
Ouija boards 39, 57, 201; as attracting parasites 170

Out-of-body experiences (OBEs) 7
Oxford University 91

Pacific islands: monotheism in 93
Paganism, Pagans 129; as tolerant 177
Pakistan 127; Indus Valley 136
Paleocontact Theory 119, 120, 127, 182
Palestinians 113
Paluga, God 181
Panspermia, theory of 104, 122
Pantheism 185
Panu, Goddess 182
Paranormal 'flaps' 140, 141
Paranormal warfare: Project Star Gate 20
Parapsychological Association, The 46
Parapsychology 17, 18, 27
Parasites
    30, 54, 57, 62, 102, 104, 110, 123, 124, 138, 141, 145, 146, 156, 170, 197;
    as aliens 105; as gods 112, 115, 116, 117, 133; as 'life-
    sucking ghosts' 117; as organized entities 107; as origin of
    vampire legends 105; as tricksters 150, 151; chronic
    fatigue syndrome 65; defense against 204, 205; feeding off
    electrical system 58, 62; feeding off events 61; limited
    mobility 109; short memories 116
Paul, St. 168; 1 Corinthians 170
Pawtuxet Valley Daily Times 48
Pele, Goddess 182
Pennsylvania: Gettysburg 28; King of Prussia 109; Philadel-
    phia 110
Personalism 88, 161, 198; vs. individualism 87, 90
Photography 32, 33, 53, 56, 105, 126
Plasma: as life-form base 107; defined 105; in photography
    56; vortices: as cause of crop circles 154
Plato 185
Plotinus 185
Poltergeists 16, 30, 45, 50, 51, 108, 110; (see also Para-
    sites) 7; Bell Witch case 114; defined 108
Polytheism 79, 91, 92, 116, 133
Possession, demonic 33, 108
Princeton University 41
Proclus 188
Providence Journal-Bulletin, The 48

Psychic: defined 108
Psychic phenomena 7, 17, 27
Psychics 17, 20, 28, 32, 46, 64, 86, 113; in Roman
    Catholic Church 78
Psychology 184; transpersonal 18
Psychotherapy 33
Purgatory 28, 29, 30, 32, 35

Quantum physics
    18, 19, 23, 34, 41, 47, 50, 126, 149; Alain Aspect
    Experiment 41; as theological principle: (*see also* Quantum
    Theology) 73; electrodynamics 41; fractals 41; gravita-
    tional singularity 84, 89; multiple worlds interpretation
    (MWI): See Multiverse 41; multiple worlds interpretation of
    42; parallel worlds: See Multiverse 49; Schroedinger's cat
    41; time paradox 45; uncertainty principle 50; wave-
    particle duality 50
Quantum theology 72, 187
Quebec: Montreal 30
Qur'an, The 22, 23, 148, 149

Rajchandra, Shrimad 168
Reality: creation of 159
Reincarnation 7; and quantum physics 167; to be escaped
    from 169
Religion: as end in itself 177; as way to know God 176, 177
Remote viewing 7, 17, 20
Rhine, Dr. Joseph B. 17
Rhine, Dr. Louisa E. 17
Rhode Island 48, 59; Providence 204; Smithfield 51
Rice University 71
Riley, Dr. Brian 27
Roman Catholic Church 28, 31, 181; ethnic affiliations
    73; Spanish Inquisition 113
Romans 207

Sagan, Dr. Carl 120
Santeria 113
Schizophrenia 30, 33
Schizotypal personality disorder 33
Scientific method, The 17, 19
Scientists: as believers in God 71, 72

Scribes, ancient and medieval 22, 23
Séances 39, 170, 201
Self: forgetfulness of: as path to fulfillment 87, 163, 193; sense
    of: as an illusion 87, 88, 161
Shamanism, shamans 86, 151, 198
Shekinah 97, 129, 140, 181
Sheppard, Susan 63
Sitchin, Zacharia 122, 123
Skeptics 15, 16, 29, 155
Sky: as father 96; gods as coming from 137, 138
Sky God 183
Slips in time and space 7, 29, 55, 86, 105, 124, 126
Sodom and Gomorrah 147
Sol Invictus 179
Spinoza, Baruch 185
Spirit orbs 13; in photography 160
Spirits 103, 105, 113, 206; as guardians 151; guardians
    among 145
Spirituality 24, 41, 177; ancestors as part of 155
St. Thomas Seminary 13
St. Vladimir Seminary 34
Statistical significance 18, 204
Stonehenge 120
Suicide 60, 61, 66
Sumerians 94, 123, 136; cuneiform 91; Kharsag Epics
    128; oldest known civilization 92
Sun: worship of 179
Sun Mother 183
Sweden: atheism in 71
Switzerland: Fribourg 120

Taoism, Taoists: female principle in 181
Tarot readers: among evangelical Christians 78
Teilhard de Chardin, Pierre 98, 99, 190
Telekinesis 17
Teleportation 13
Tennessee: Adams 114; Robertson County 114, 115
Terrorists 113, 159
Tetragrammaton, The 147
Texas 158; Houston 71; Paluxy River 125
The Observer 51
Theosis 188

Tillich, Rev. Paul 185
Time: as function of consciousness 167
Torah, The 22, 23, 97
Trinity College 35

Ubuntu: African principle of 95, 166
UFOs 6, 7, 86, 124, 140, 153, 160; photography 126
Unity, The 86, 94, 139, 150, 192, 207; and all possibilities
    89; and sense of self 161; as fulfillment of individuality
    88; as indiscriminate 165; as path to God 75, 87; as
    ultimate motivation 85; as undercurrent of reality 82; at
    Creation 84; breakage of 90, 99, 108, 112; experiencing
    199; love discovered in 201
University of Chicago 72, 92
University of Connecticut 36, 46
University of London 27
University of Waterloo 97
University of Wisconsin 158
Utah: bizarre fossils 125

Vampire legends 104
Vermont 106; Burlington 31
Virgin Mary 23, 149; as expression of Divine Mother 181
Visualization: in meditation 197; power of 204
von Däniken, Erich 119, 120, 121, 122, 123, 127
Voodoo 113

Wadhams Hall Seminary 33, 34
Warren, Lorraine 32, 35
West Virginia 140, 204; Parkersburg: Blennerhasset Island 62
Wever, Dr. Rutger 34, 50
White, Dr. Rhea 7, 27
Wicca, Wiccans 142
Wisconsin: kangaroo sightings 124
Wolf, Dr. Fred Alan 41

Yahweh 129, 140, 142, 148

Zoroaster 179
Zoroastrianism, Zoroastrians 142
Zulus 166; oral history 93

The Author

PAUL F. ENO has been an investigator of paranormal phenomena for over 35 years. A graduate of two seminaries and holder of a degree in philosophy, he is an award-winning journalist and a former news editor at The Providence Journal-Bulletin. Articles by him have appeared in national magazines in America and Britain, and he has appeared on the Discovery, History and Travel Channels. He is a popular talk-show guest, and presents programs on the paranormal all over North America. He and his family live in Rhode Island.

Also by Paul F. Eno:
(Available from New River Press)
The Best of Times (1992)
Faces at the Window (1998)
First-Hand Accounts of the Paranormal in Southern New England
Footsteps in the Attic (2002)
More First-Hand Accounts of the Paranormal in New England
Rhode Island: A Genial History (2005)
(with Glenn Laxton)

Visit www.newriverpress.com or your favorite bookseller

(From Oxford University Press, London)
"William Blackstone"
in American National Biography

(From Pamphlet Publications, Chicago)
The Occult (1977)*
Preventive Medicine for the Occult (1979)*

*out of print

Coming from New River Press
for the Holiday Season, 2006

Letters

from Legends

and the
Incredible Interviews
that Inspired Them

by award-winning celebrity journalist

Marian Christy

These previously unpublished letters to the author
by major figures in government, show business and
the media, based on her eye-opening interviews with
them, will keep you glued to this amazing book from
beginning to end. Included are Richard Nixon,
Jerry Lewis, Tom Brokaw, Yoko Ono,
Corretta Scott King, Dan Rather, Joan Crawford,
Jacqueline Kennedy Onassis, and many, many more!

ISBN: 1-891724-07-X
ISBN 13: 978-1-891724-07-7

Coming from New River Press
for the Holiday Season, 2006

Shadows

on my Shift

Real-Life Stories of a
Psychic EMT

Sherri Lee Devereau

Emergency medical workers expect to see dead people
in their line of work, but what makes this Phoenix,
Arizona, EMT different is her ability to communicate
with those who are just starting their "journey to the
other side." The messages she receives, and how she
conveys them to grieving loved ones without causing
more pain, make for a
uniquely touching and dramatic story!

www.shadowsonmyshift.com

ISBN: 1-891724-08-8
ISBN 13: 978-1-891724-08-4

Now available from New River Press!

41 SIGNS of Hope

By Dave Kane

From New England talk-show host Dave Kane,
father of Nick O'Neill, youngest of the 100 victims of the
disastrous 2003 Station nightclub fire in Rhode Island,
comes a book full of hope that our loved ones do not die.
After the passing of this gifted young man came a series of
amazing "coincidences" based on the number 41, his

favc 133 E59

incident   n

his p Eno, Paul F.
Turning home : God, ghosts &
human destiny
Looscan ADU CIRC
09/11

ISBN: 1-891724-05-3
ISBN 13: 978-1-891724-05-3